KALEIDOSCOPE

absurdly short stories of traveling and
unraveling

CHRISTINA QUIST

For Jackson, Dylan, Evangeline, Hudson and Ethan, my original Big Five. The best stories I have are you.

For Kevin, who thought moving to South Africa was a good idea.

For my grandma Hovda, who said she always liked my writing.

For Ocean View, a city on a hill.

Though many thought she had lost her wits, I knew that she had found her soul.

Julian of Norwich

Contents

Preface

A note on terms used in this book: Within my scope of limited understanding, I tried my utmost to honor the many races, ethnicities and nations within the diverse nation of South Africa. The terms Black, White, Coloured, Khoisan and Indian are cultural, ethnic and racial demographics within South Africa. More is explained in the following chapters.

Thank you to my South African friends who patiently continue to teach me about the complexities of your country, as I continue to learn.

Introduction

> At the height of laughter, the universe is flung
> into a kaleidoscope of new possibilities.
>
> Jean Huston

My neighbor's name is Bing Crosby. She has 47 tortoises, three weiner dogs and is a taser-carrying member of our local Neighborhood Watch. How I got here is a bit complicated. Somewhere in my suburban-middle-class-soccer-mom phase, we moved to Cape Town, South Africa where I'm still a suburban middle-class soccer mom but in a slightly more life-changing context.

For one, Bing is real. She has an "official" name but few people know it. I'm one of them, but I'm not going to say because then I wouldn't have a neighbor called Bing Crosby who rides a scooter to fight brush fires and chases down undesirables in the neighborhood.

Somewhere around age 39, I got sick on the merry-go-round of life. If I wasn't teaching school, I was clipping coupons and running kids to soccer games. If I wasn't fretting about my pants size I was driving through Starbucks for a Frappuccino. I was an upstanding citizen of my local church. I attended women's groups, volunteered for nursery duty and hot glued AWANA patches on my kids' vests for every Bible challenge they accomplished.

We've been married for more than 25 years, my husband Kevin and I. We have four boys-Jackson, Dylan, Hudson, and Ethan. Our only daughter, Evangeline, is smack in the middle of the boys. Hudson and Ethan came last, as a pièce de résistance. Surprise! Numbers #4 and #5 are a tandem pair. It's one thing to have a large family. But once you have five kids, you enter into that other dimension of homeschooling, driving extended minivans and winning spelling bees. We had five kids in a span of six years. The first half of my life was a glorious monument to motherhood coupled with survival tactics that I can only assume will require intensive therapy for my adult children.

Now, we live in a country where the nearest Starbucks is 18 hours away. I don't own a clothes dryer. We buy our electricity at the grocery store and pay someone to guard our car while we go into the shopping mall. Segregation was mandatory until about 20 years ago and remains so in word and deed. There was nothing wrong with our lives the way we were headed. It was perfectly in line with the cultural expectation.

Have you ever had that gnawing feeling that maybe there's more to life than just surviving it? That raising good kids is more than hoping they get into a good college and don't swear a whole lot? What are we here for? What am I supposed to be doing here, with this family, with this time

I've been given? How do I experience life? Who has the right to tell me that I must conform to society's version of cozy and comfortable?

There had to be more. I wasn't hard-wired for this lifestyle, that much I knew. We wanted to know a radical God, the God of crazy stories that are not past tense but are alive and active right now. We wanted to be the ones telling the crazy stories, not just repeating someone else's story. We wanted our own stories. All or nothing. Life was God's narrative lived through us, but we were a pretty boring story. I needed to see what that could look like, not what it shouldn't look like according to keepers of the tradition.

Life was meant to be lived in the wild, open spaces of infinite possibility, not confined to a box of safety and security while the story raged around us.

To make a long story short...we sold everything that wouldn't fit into suitcases and bought seven one-way tickets to South Africa.

The process is MESSY, in fact, it's downright embarrassing.

My perspective at the time of this story has shifted and changed. Things I said then, I cringe at now. Decisions I made then, I might not make now. But that's the thing with time. We learn retroactively.

Some stories might make you shudder with fear, some might make you cringe with embarrassment, others might invite you to cry in compassion. There is no right or wrong to our stories, there is only growth and learning. Who I was in my first year of leaving the US is not who I am after five years and I'm not yet who I will be in 15 years.

These life lessons aren't just about my delightful neighbor, Bing Crosby. They are gritty and filthy, heartbreaking and embarrassing because they are all living and active. The thing is, when you throw open your windows to let in the light, a few other things are bound to buzz in too.

Sometimes I look at life like we are the fractals of color inside a kaleidoscope. Depending on how the light reflects the color, the pattern and shape of the fractals look differently. The kaleidoscope turns and the fractals tumble and fall and form again. The light pours through and the beauty is never boring. That's what these stories are—a mixture of time and places, moods, and thoughts, people and events. All these things tumble around in one unpredictable, beautiful picture called life. This is a collection of thoughts, experiences, trials, embarrassments, growth, and absolute trust.

We traded our comforts and security for the wild unknown. These are the things that shaped us then and continue to shape us now. All of these things have been tumbling around in the unpredictable, beautiful picture called my life. Welcome to my kaleidoscope.

These are some of our colorful stories.

The Unwinding

*Though your destination is not yet clear You
can trust the promise of this opening;
Unfurl yourself into the grace of beginning
That is at one with your life's desire.*

John O'Donohue

ONCE UPON A TIME, my grandparents managed a primitive summer campground in Side Lake, Minnesota. Rustic wood cabins huddled around the lake under an arena of pine trees in a secluded area far from civilization. Local churches dropped their kids here each week by the busload. A few cabins belonged to seasonal neighbors but other than that, the summer belonged to us. We spent long, hot days in the cool lake water, tanning to dark brown; our waterlogged skin in a permanent state of glorious wrinkle.

The female-only saunas rested on a sandy path between the lake and base camp. Not luxury saunas mind you. Only the kitchen and director's cabin had indoor plumbing and running water. These saunas were a testament to a regional Scandinavian tradition and a very low budget.

My cousins and I gathered here to sweat and chatter before bedtime. Inside, black wooden benches with the occasional splinter surrounded a hot stove piled with igneous sauna stones. One brave soul volunteered to venture close enough to the stove to toss a ladleful of water onto the rocks and quickly retreat to the benches before being seared like Japanese tuna. The rest of us gulped in hot, steamy air that tasted like the smell of iron ore.

At the point of near suffocation, we would fling open the wooden door and burst into the cool, summer air. Hot steam rose from our skin, as we sprinted down the sandy walkway, out onto the rickety metal dock and dove into the cold, dark lake water below; four ghostly apparitions in purple and pink modest, one-piece, camp counselor approved bathing suits.

Of course, my cousins, being pesky boys, fished during the day and tied up a string of prized fish directly underneath the diving board. Let me tell you, there's nothing quite like a string of Northern Pike thrashing in the dark water to make you want to walk on water. We had no idea what awaited us under that mysterious surface, but it didn't matter. We were much too hot and bothered to stay one more minute in the suffocating hot box.

That's my life. Right there.

For the first 19 years of our marriage, we lived a "normal" Christian life thinking that "this" is what it's all about. We were living in small-town Ohio, teaching at a small, private Christian high school.

Jackson, Dylan, and Hudson played soccer on traveling teams, which took the word "travel" quite literally. We sometimes drove to Washington D.C. to play one game. Evangeline played on a club volleyball team and Ethan played the piano thanks to some covert bribery because we needed some musicians in this family. Driver's education, big families, homework, lesson plans, and church-life was ridiculously busy and empty.

Between Saturday night and Monday morning, God could be found at an address with a steeple. On the other days of the week, I was my own lord. I didn't need God, except when I needed a backup plan. It was my go-to-world of managed, compartmentalized faith and belief. God was safely contained inside my box, neatly stored away in a doctrine of original sin and knee-length shorts.

There were dividing lines and protective barriers, labels and mislabels. As long as I kept everything in my neat, tidy, controllable row, God didn't pay me much attention, nor I, Him. Life was…well, boring.

Where was this Jesus that changed the world and faced the Roman empire and the religious system? I wanted to live my life following *that* Jesus. Where was the awe, the astonishment, the whispering reminders of an ongoing story? I had somehow ended up with a suburban God who scheduled play dates and politely applauded special music in church.

The "American Dream" was no longer enough. This house with multiple bedrooms, this car-pooling to soccer games, this church on Sundays, the stressful holidays, the traditions we were manipulated into upholding year after year after year; it was time for a change.

3

I lived for 39 years in this box, and I couldn't take it any longer. I had to break free and make a run for it. Don't get me wrong, there's nothing wrong with the American dream. It just wasn't what we were supposed to be doing. I had been sitting in the sauna too long and I was bloated with busyness and starved for purpose. Even though it started off great, it was now a sweaty, claustrophobic mess and it was time to start listening to the voice inside.

Kevin, thankfully, felt the same, and restlessness and hopefulness started to grow in us both. Our unfolding began with questions. Agitating questions that bore no fruitful answers from mere mortals. We already knew that the certainty of answers was unsatisfying. It is the unknowing of things that leads to a deeper mystery.

For years, I tried to suppress the questions because I was afraid of who I might become if I continued to question. Instead, I discovered that mystery and unknowing was a gift, and the letting go was a journey that required blindly moving into the beautiful unknown.

So we ran.

It felt like we jumped into the deep end with our eyes closed, only to discover that not only were we not drowning, but we could actually breathe here. This is where I found myself. Just beyond the point where you can still see the surface, the space where the darkness is inky black. It's been a process to learn to see again, to adjust our eyes to the dark, to wait while our vision crept into focus.

But when we wait long enough, we can see that what we thought was missing, has been there all along. It's us. Unconfined and captivated by freedom, God's transcendence enveloping us. Seeing us.

Don't get me wrong, I'm not saying that you have to leave everything and move to Africa. Only that you believe that you could move to Africa. Or Portland, or Kosovo or any place, metaphysical or geographical, where you can see people, and feel pain and taste joy. Places where you can experience life apart from any political party line or denomination.

On the journey, we learned that liberation doesn't come without risk. When Moses led the Israelites out of slavery from Egypt, the Red Sea wasn't already parting in preparation for their escape. The Israelites faced their oppressors on one side, in hot pursuit thanks to a humiliating bout with the plagues. They faced the Red Sea on the other. It wasn't until they were squeezed in the middle with nowhere to go that the escape route opened up, right where they least expected. It felt the same for us.

We also discovered that extreme life makeovers are not a Disney movie. There is no fairy tale ending or musical soundtrack. It's stinking messy. There was an ever-present jury box inside my head demanding judgment. Confronting this inner dialogue that threatened to take me down has never really gone away. It just holds court less often. I have learned that the wild that rages inside me can only be answered by the wild unknown. I am called to echo it.

Living like this has humbled me, shaped me, taught me, flattened and inspired me. The old me is no longer here. Since the day we left the US, I knew life would be different.

I remember wondering if this is what the explorers felt like when they sailed from the motherland to prove that the world was round. I knew in my heart that it was the right thing to do, but there was still that nagging thought that if we're wrong, this could end very, very badly.

2

Bread Crumb Jesus

What you seek is seeking you.

Rumi

WHAT MADE us choose South Africa? It chose us. In each one of us, there's a thread that weaves its way through our lives, leaving little clues about who we are and who we are to become. It's like God leaves little bread crumbs on a trail and when we stop and look, we can see the path before us.

When I was a little girl growing up in Phoenix, I owned a book of children's fairy tales, from which I'm fairly traumatized. I hated the tale of Hansel and Gretel and how the evil witch lured little kids into the forest by leaving bread crumbs on a path to her house made of candies. Once inside, she shoved them into the oven.

Who reads these to kids? Hansel and Gretel should be rated R for violence, kidnapping, and psychological terror. This story had to be someone's idea of deterring childhood obesity as if filling me with terror could sway me from carb-loading on my way to a house of Swedish fish.

When I read the fairy tale book with my grandma, she would retell the story to me. In her version, when Hansel and Gretel followed the bread crumbs through the forest, they found the gingerbread house covered in candies where the kind granny wore a pink velour tracksuit and invited them in for hot soup and bread.

I wonder if Hansel and Gretel subconsciously manifested a fear in Christendom that said, "Don't follow that clue, that bread crumb, you never know where it could lead." Maybe it will lead to an ambush by a wicked witch with a penchant for cannibalism.

In other words, don't trust yourself. Stay in the suburbs where houses are in a cul-de-sac and you'll never have to face what's waiting for you in the woods.

However, what if the bread crumbs are there for us? And the house of candy awaits? If you believe in a loving God who has been awaiting your arrival with a hot bowl of soup, there is immense freedom in following the path to discovering more of your story.

It's a story we are invited to co-create. It's not so much a life plan as it is a poem. A plan leaves little room for surprise or divine sabotage, but a poem is curiosity and passion with room for interpretation.

Looking back, I can see the bread crumbs and trace the winding presence for 20 years before I could conceive of this possibility. There are the crumbs and clues we don't always follow but we notice their presence every now and again when we pay attention. It's there with us, all of us, like a scavenger hunt which takes you on a discovery, and when you follow, it will keep leading.

My crumbs began in 1990. Fresh out of high school and bloated with my own knowledge, I attended college at a tiny Bible school in Chicago. News of Nelson Mandela's release from South Africa's Pollsmoor prison hit the front page of the Chicago Tribune, back when the news was printed on paper and holding it turned your fingers black with ink. I was an 18-year old freshman with dreams of becoming a journalist.

The name Nelson Mandela was synonymous with "terrorist" in my circles. Yet, the news outlets and newspaper seemed jubilant at his release. Mandela, and then president F.W. de Klerk, shared the Nobel Peace Prize. At that time, I had no idea the turmoil South Africans were enduring as they held their breath in suspense for their country's future.

A curiosity was born and the birth of this new republic ran parallel to the birth of my own independence. This began my inexplicable connection to a country I'd never visited and to people I'd never met.

A few years later, I read *Cry the Beloved Country* and *Too Late the Phalarope* by South African author Alan Paton. Words like Afrikaans, Soweto, District 6, Robben Island, Steve Biko, Shaka Zulu, proteas, and fynbos lingered in my mind and swirled around like imaginary places and people.

WHEN IT CAME time to choose a language for my linguistics class project, I chose to study Zulu simply because the word sounded cool. Little did I know that someday I would hear it in person and meet the Zulus who speak it. *Bread crumb.*

The next few years were a blur of American dreaminess. Marriage, house, kids, job…but every time I heard mention of South Africa, a little spark would light in my heart. *Bread crumb*.

In 2003, a missionary couple visited the church we attended. They were from Free State, South Africa. They were looking for volunteers. Oh, how we lost control of our imaginations! At this stage, both Kevin and I felt a tug toward South Africa. As often happens with married couples, who is to say if it was just sheer mimesis, or if we were both hearing from God?

Either way, we dreamed in ways that our context and exposure would allow, like thinking that Kevin could teach music and math to people in grass huts. My heart bounced along with possibility and wonder. I didn't even know where Free State was located, I knew it was in South Africa and that was all that mattered. We jumped through hoops and logic to try to maneuver this dream into reality.

We had five young kids. The twins were just two years old and the sleep-deprived brain fog was just beginning to lift. During the day I folded laundry and dreamed of our life in South Africa. At night, I spent precious sleeping hours dialing up AOL trying to research more about this mysterious location.

A friend of mine caught our vision and passion. She was in the throes of mission board approval. We dreamed together of raising kids under the South African sun. She had experience navigating the gauntlet of mission board approvals.

At the time there was only one way (in my mind) to get to South Africa and it met with a mental barrier—the approval of a mission board. This was the way missions was done in the past. It was all we knew. It's what real missionaries did. They got approval by a governing board who decided who could and couldn't go. Then you took a family photo that later becomes a fridge magnet.

I suggested that we skip the mission board approval stage, recruit enough friends to financially support us and just go. I was fairly certain I would not pass the mission board approval exam. I still owned Def Leppard cassette tapes for crying out loud.

I was informed by well-meaning people that this was not the way one moves one's family across the country to deepest, darkest Africa. To do so without the approval and permission of a governing body of well-meaning people and administrators was insanity. There was paperwork and policies to consider. One doesn't just up and leave the greatest nation on earth to move to a third-world country.

We didn't move to Free State. But another idea was born— the 'trusting God to provide' idea. The 'skipping the tedious fundraising' idea, the 'wait three years to go so you can raise enough funds to survive' idea. All good ideas, just not for us. The inspiration to just pick up and go would never fully disappear. *Bread crumb.*

About once a month or so we would find another bread crumb, a clue on the scavenger hunt of possibility. Kevin would call me when he randomly saw a car in a central Ohio Walmart parking lot with South African flags on the rearview mirror, or when a song or story would trigger a reminder about this country.

The call to another life was there, floating around us, beckoning.

3

Did You Take That into Consideration?

In order to arrive at what you do not know
You must go by a way which is the way of
    ignorance.

In order to possess what you do not possess
You must go by the way of dispossession.

T.S. Eliot

WHEN MAKING LIFE-CHANGING DECISIONS, I've learned that there is a grace that buffers us from overwhelming thoughts. It allows us to take into consideration how our decisions affect others, but prods us into our given direction, regardless.

Fortunately, we were in such a protective bubble during this stage, somehow both divinely mute and blind, only able to respond to the summoning of life outside its current offering. That means we didn't even pay attention to the scuttlebutt and gossip surrounding our choice, which we only discovered years later.

There is a cognitive knowing that makes decisions based on logic and rationale. But that is limited to what we know. The thing is, we didn't know what we didn't know. So how could we make a decision based on myopic perceptions and limited understanding?

Providentially, we also have a knowing that is intuitive, and that knowledge must be given substantial consideration. We didn't know how we were going to survive in South Africa. We only knew on a deeper level that superseded cognitive explanation, that God was much bigger than we allowed.

As it turns out, a life change doesn't have to be a big, "Aha" moment. It can be one hundred little moments. I don't even know how the book got into my hands, but somehow I found myself reading a book called, *The Hole in Our Gospel* by Richard Stearns. This book, combined with *Crazy Love* by Francis Chan, started to accelerate the unraveling process. In Stearns' book, he spoke of a non-profit organization called Living Hope in Cape Town, South Africa, founded by John Thomas, that was garnering international attention for HIV/AIDS work.

There was a paragraph in the book about John meeting President George Bush in the White House to accept awards for his humanitarian work, along with a short biography and his email address. My mind became more than a little unhinged. What if we, just Kevin and I, visited this organization? Was that even a thing? I mean, could we just try on missions work to check the fit?

Maybe I'd just email this John Thomas guy and see if he

responded. If this trip was meant to be, he'll return my email, happily inviting us to visit. If he was a normal person, he'd delete it and block my address because I was clearly a stalker.

Less than 24 hours later, an email appeared in my inbox from John Thomas himself. "Dear Christina, We would love to have you and your husband visit us in Cape Town. What dates would suit you best?" That escalated quickly! We didn't even own passports.

Yet, somehow, we learned the ropes of international travel. We applied for passports, booked our flights and secured accommodation with Living Hope's team house. School was nearly finished for the summer which gave us the free time required to fly across the world to live with complete strangers.

Thankfully, both sets of grandparents stepped in to help with our five kids for what would be the longest separation in our family's history. I typed a notebook of instructions, color-coded with play-by-play precision, detailing which child should be where at what time, what they liked to eat and what they wanted to be when they grew up. I'm pretty sure I even typed a letter to each of them in the event that we died in a fiery plane crash.

Oh, the packing! It would be winter in South Africa so should we bring winter coats or malaria pills? What exactly were these African diseases everyone kept warning us about and why did everyone keep insisting we needed shots?

We booked flights with a 12 hour layover in London since I'd always wanted to visit London and this seemed as good a time as any.

We had zero clues about international travel, visas, London, those red telephone booths (shocking den of iniquity), what happens to your ankles after a 34 hour flight, or exactly what heartache feels like when you're 8,000 miles away from your kids.

WE WERE ONLY in Cape Town a few days before something started to feel familiar. We met lovely people of all colors and backgrounds. We saw informal settlements, wealthy neighborhoods, homeless shelters, and stunning views of ocean waves and mountain vistas.

The Mother City called to us in whispers from her people. They seemed to know that we were on a spiritual journey. Here, the spiritual and physical realms are not yet separated as harshly as in the Western mind. South Africa compelled us with a heart-wrenching invitation to put down roots in her soil and sit in her classroom.

Although we brought only a few souvenirs when we returned from the two-week 'scouting' trip, we did bring back an invitation to return to serve as volunteers with Living Hope. I distinctly remember our meeting with Tim and Natasha, young volunteer coordinators for the non-profit organization we came to visit.

Tim is a tall, blonde engineer from the United States who spoke deliberately with fully formed sentences. He liked spreadsheets, I could tell. Natasha is a white South African whose Afrikaans accent has been distilled by years of living aboard. Both look like models.

During our visits to various areas of Cape Town, including a community called Ocean View, I marveled at the way

Natasha moved in and out of people groups, making herself comfortable, sitting cross-legged on a dusty cement floor amongst a circle of young kids. I could see that she genuinely loves people and is passionate about her country.

On our last day in Cape Town, we sat with Tim and Natasha on the balcony of a restaurant in Noordhoek, eating wood-fired pizza covered in feta cheese and bitter lettuce. The sun warmed us in a clear blue sky on that winter day in August.

We talked about our visit and summarized our experiences. Had another couple been sitting in front of us, I'm not sure we would have felt the same way, but there was such a common passion between us, a camaraderie that went beyond recruiting for an organization.

Tim asked us if we would consider moving to South Africa. I had rehearsed the answer to this question in my mind because I somehow knew it was coming. I wanted to yell, "Of course, we will come to live here! My heart is at home here. I feel like I belong. We belong!"

I glanced at Kevin who was giving me the side-eye. Instead, I said, "We will pray about it."

If ever there was a Christian stall tactic, that was it. My heart already knew the answer. I think Tim and Natasha did too. We had found a missing piece to our puzzle.

WE RETURNED to Ohio later that week and excitedly told our kids what we had seen, learned and experienced. We didn't once mention the possibility of moving. To this day, no one remembers who said it, but as we perched on our bed while sorting through pictures and African treats, one of the boys yelled, "Pack your bags, kids, I think we are moving to Africa."

There was much to take into consideration.

We could not legally seek employment in South Africa because a volunteer visa doesn't permit foreigners to work. That meant no income. Zero. Zilch. Eight thousand miles from even a minimum wage job. Yes, we took that into consideration. Pretty much every waking hour of the day.

My family was close. Until my sister broke ranks and moved to Texas, we all lived in the same vicinity of small-town Ohio. Family picnics involved competitive games of kickball where everyone knew that Grandma would be the first to cheat.

Holidays, church, soccer games, basketball games, volleyball games, spelling bees, band concerts, birthdays, births of at least 12 nieces and nephews... all spent together.

In the course of finalizing our decision, the only five voices we took into consideration were sitting on my bed. The grace would extend to them, take them into the transition and walk with them. They would leave friends, family, athletic teams, and the only state they had ever called home. Ethan and Hudson were 11-years-old, Evangeline was 13, Dylan,15 and Jackson, 17.

By all accounts, we should have been doing college visits and SAT prep. Was it easy? Never. Was it pretty? More often than not, no. Was it their journey? Yes. And for each one, we tried to allow their individual expression of this journey to come forth. They didn't just play a part in our story. They needed to write their own chapters.

In the "old days," it was said that missionaries used to bring their coffins with them to Africa to be buried because there was no going back. That wasn't us. We had the Internet and could hop on a flight and be back in a solid 26 hours.

People often think Cape Town is the bush of the Serengeti. When we announced we wanted to move to South Africa, some people assumed we would send monthly updates via a glass bottle. Others threw us a farewell before we ever left. Given the amount of silence between us, I think they mistook the announcement for an obituary.

There were the things we needed to take into consideration, but those weren't the things that made our decision.

4

What Have You Done?

You know, sometimes all you need is twenty-
seconds of insane courage. Just literally
twenty seconds of just embarrassing
bravery. And I promise you, something
great will come of it.

Benjamin Mee

FIRST TIME MOMS are the sweetest, the way they think
everyone wants to hear about their baby's latest development.
That's what we did. We talked about South Africa, apartheid,
civil rights, and our desire to visit like a first time mom who
has just seen her first ultrasound.

I'm not sure that everyone in our mostly white social network
in Ohio appreciated our running lectures on racism, oppression and the white minority government that brutalized a
majority black population.

As teachers, we sometimes turned our lessons into discus-
sions about civil rights, Woolworth's sit-ins and the power

struggle that could have been a civil war. This is pretty impressive considering that Kevin taught pre-Algebra.

As a baby grows, it demands more space and energy. By nine months, the mother is more than ready for the baby to be born, even though she has cherished each stage of development. I've yet to meet a woman who has wanted to be pregnant forever, although, I have met several who have given it a good go.

The immense desire to give birth eventually becomes so intense that it demands a response. New life must come forth. So it was for us. We could not *not* do it.

Between family and friends, we had an immense support system and a loving nest from which to take flight. We lived in a glorious bubble that kept us insulated from negative comments or critical judgment, only seeing adventure and an untethered dream coming into possibility.

Reality hit home, however, when we gave away most of our furniture and moved in with friends, mainly because there was no turning back. We lived with them for four months and then ultimately moved into my parent's basement.

It was supposed to be for a few months but ended up lasting for a year while we sorted through visas and overseas accommodations. They lived in a two-bedroom, one-bathroom house. That's nine people in a two-bedroom house. One bathroom. One. Thankfully, the majority of the occupants were boys so they could make use of the forest behind the house.

The material purging was yet another stage of the birthing process. We gave away everything that wouldn't fit into suitcases, including our beloved minivan with dual sliding doors, DVD players and stow-and-go seating. Someone initially gave us this amazing minivan so it felt only right to give it to someone else. As it turned out, the son of the family we gifted it to became our first financial supporter and most understanding friend.

We finally purchased seven one-way tickets to South Africa with a layover in London. Looking ahead, South Africa held the great unknown, adventure, and anticipation. Looking back were parents, brothers, my sister, cousins, and friends. The path to desire was an ever-painful place scattered with abandoned people and abandoned dreams.

Nevertheless, we knew that if we took the pain we might inflict on our loved ones into too great a consideration, we would live in a place of self-sacrifice that would breed regret. Yet, there was a grace that wrapped around all who left and all who stayed. This grace connected us because Lord knows, airport scenes are the worst.

AFTER 27-HOURS OF TRAVELING, we arrived in Cape Town, all seven of us and our 21 pieces of luggage. It was June. It was winter. It was cold and raining. Tim and Natasha met us at the airport and helped collect our immense pile of luggage.

We headed to the furnished house we rented where an estate agent met us and used words like crockery and cutlery but we are all so very tired. We nodded and signed the paperwork. After everyone left, we sat down in our new house in a suburb of Cape Town.

I looked around and noticed the owner's decor style. My guess was a 65-year old single lady, judging by the family of wooden cats painted in festive colors sitting by the fireplace. They reminded me of Cinco de Mayo. I didn't know yet that not having legitimate TexMex nachos will cause a mild family crisis in a few weeks. There were dishes in the cupboards, and an electric tea kettle we had yet to learn to use.

There were electric blankets on each bed because we didn't know yet that the country didn't have central heating. But they did have single-pane windows and wide open drafts. There was a pool outside and something called a braai area. There was no coffee maker. Plot twist. There was no coffee maker! I wish someone would've mentioned this detail.

It was raining and cold. No one said Cape Town would be cold. The rain and wind howled and I mean *howled* relentlessly. It never stopped. All day. All night. It sounded like the single pane windows were rattling right out of their single pane frames. But alas, after house-sharing and living in my parents' basement, to have our own bed was downright glorious.

As the sun set over the Fish Hoek valley on our first day in South Africa, house lights and streets lights began to turn on. Luckily, Kevin figured out how to drive our rental car with a manual transmission while sitting on the right-hand side of the car yet, driving on the left-hand side of the road.

Because it was Friday and every Friday night was family pizza night, he ordered a pepperoni pizza from a small place that advertised wood-fired pizza. Little did we know, when the pizza place said 'pepperoni' they actually meant salami. It wasn't bad, it was just different. (For the next three years we would be unable to locate a proper pepperoni pizza).

We huddled around the heater, wrapped in blankets, eating pizza while we noticed the stars. Even the constellations were different. There's a whole thing with the Southern Hemisphere and constellations. I downloaded an app for the iPad so we could figure out which stars we were seeing. We ate salami pizza and marveled at the Southern Cross and Telescopium. It was the end of June. It was winter. The house made strange noises and things smelled weird.

It was only after my sleep-deprived mind began to mull over the events of the last 48 hours that I began to realize the magnitude of what had just happened. There were new words for commonplace objects like serviette and robot and boot and brinjal. There were people living in shacks next to people who lived in homes, like ours.

There were exotic languages, winter traditions, cold buildings, and rooibos tea. All these things had an air of excitement and exploration mixed with intimidation and wave after wave of homesickness.

Even if we rethought the decision and decided we were crazy and should not be permitted to make major life decisions, it was done. We no longer owned a vehicle. Most of our furniture was gone and the rest was being stored indefinitely in the homes, cellars, and garages of relatives.

The funds we saved for this move took a hit with a double deposit and first month's rent. We had enough to survive for a couple of months and God would surely take care of the future.

I imagined the financial supporters we had when we left would be sure to tell their friends what we were doing. When stories of the work in South Africa began to spread, the financial support would surely increase. Or so we thought...

For now, we were much too poor to be able to fly back, should we change our minds. We were much too far away for someone to fly over and give us a pep talk. There was only us, all seven of us in various stages of grief and excitement.

As the first night closed around us, we watched the valley light up with twinkling stars, screeching car alarms and police sirens filling the background like white noise. There were new smells, new sights and different spellings for familiar words in an unfamiliar place where almost no one knew that we had arrived.

5

The Ugly American

When you travel, remember that a foreign
country is not designed to make you
comfortable. It is designed to make its own
people comfortable.

Clifton Fadiman

I FANCIED MYSELF A PEACE-LOVING, calm-under-pressure type of Midwest gal. Until this particular day. After three weeks in our new house, we hadn't yet gotten our phone bill straightened out which meant no service which meant no Internet for nearly a month.

Undoubtedly, this just confirmed to my American friends that we were indeed living in the Kalahari, squatting in our loincloths, scratching primitive communication symbols in the dirt. I had run out of patience and understanding. I was done with cross-cultural sensitivity. It was time to take care of this phone bill once and for all.

Kevin and I went to the mall, where the grocery store and

phone company were located. He chose to go to the grocery store while I marched into Telkom, the country's one and only phone company.

If I calculated correctly, I should finish before he even got through the bread aisle. You see, on our first phone bill, they overcharged us by about 700 Rands. ($70).

I took my phone bill and passport into the office, expecting customer service. I walked up to the customer service counter and explained that I needed to have my bill adjusted because there was a mistake.

"Oh, you need to call Telkom. We have a direct line."

The nice lady gestured me over to a small table with a phone on it. "Call from there," she said.

Wait a minute. I was calling Telkom FROM Telkom? What kind of phone company has a phone line to itself? This was not going to go well.

Here was the problem: I speak English and they were speaking English. Yet, we couldn't understand each other over the phone. This American accent was harder to decipher than you would think. I needed to see LIPS when conversing so I could hear what was being said. No visuals, no hearing.

Over the phone, there were lots of words on repeat like pardon? sorry? hello? Sometimes when I couldn't understand the question I just said yes and hope I hadn't agreed to a felony.

I called anyway. Call #1. I explain that the bill was wrong.

First hurdle: I called it a telephone bill. It was a TELE-PHONY bill.

Gave phone number, passport number, address. Explained again that we didn't order the deluxe package with caller ID, voice mail, etc. We only used the phone line for Internet access.

We only made 3 phone calls last month. Two were accidents. We didn't need CallBlocker. We didn't have friends yet, let alone enemies.

Transferred to someone else. Gave phone number, passport number, address, cell number, and last known zip code.

"My bill is wrong. Can you please adjust it?"

"You have to cancel those services first," said customer rep #2.

"I didn't order these services. We just ordered the most basic package."

"Yes, you did. We don't give you packages you don't order."

Transferred.

Gave phone number, passport number, address, cell phone number, last known zip code, birthday, and anniversary.

"Hello. How can I help you?"

Again, same story.

"You need to call Telkom. Press numbah waan and thain numbah thrrree."

WAIT A MINUTE!!! I WAS CALLING THE PHONE COMPANY FROM INSIDE THE PHONE COMPANY ONLY TO BE TOLD I NEED TO CALL THE PHONE COMPANY??!

Yes.

Transferred.

Gave address, passport number, address, cell phone number, birthday, dress size, and name of the family pet. And a few nonverbal expletives.

Transferred. Again. Again. Again.

One HOUR AND 30 MINUTES LATER…I WAS STILL INSIDE THE PHONE COMPANY!

The only thing I accomplished was pressing the phone so hard into my head that my temples were numb. My ears were throbbing. I thought I had cauliflower ear.

In the meantime, Kevin had enough time to do a bit of grocery shopping and I found him practicing his isiXhosa in the mall.

"How did it go?" he happily clicked at me.

"I'm not sure. I have to call tomorrow," I fumed.

I got home later that evening and found the phone service completely disconnected.

6

Lost in Translation

Words are the source of misunderstandings.

Antoine de Saint-Exupéry

I WAS EVER SO grateful to my new friend, Karen. She was a highly outgoing South African mom of little boys who helped us find a home, introduced us to a handy Internet device called a 'dongle' and plied us with donuts that claimed to be donuts but lied.

When she called one afternoon to say she would be over 'just now' we were excited to hear the news, albeit surprised by the short notice. Like any good mother, I thrust our five kids into turbo cleaning mode with wild-eyed instructions, shoving the big stuff into closets and underneath beds. I wished my house was perpetually cleaned and organized, ready for guests, but alas, no. That was just not who I was as a person.

"When is Karen coming?" my husband asked, trying to gauge the endurance factor needed for my cleaning blitzkrieg.

"She said 'just now.' I think that means she was in the neighborhood. Should be any minute."

One hour passed. The kids thought I had made up the arrival of our guest as a ruse to get the house cleaned. Two hours. Now I was beginning to worry. Had she lost her way? Or worse, *gasp* had she been hijacked? What if something had gone terribly awry? The family waited. I would call, but since I couldn't figure out how to get our phone connected, it was no use.

After three hours, the doorbell rang and I heard Karen's voice. Whew! She's here, alive! The house breathed a collective sigh of relief.

"What's the matter?" she said, at the sight of my panicked face.

"We were so worried about you. You said you were going to be here just now and it's three hours later."

"Ohhhh", she said. "You don't say 'just now'?"

"Yes, I say 'just now' when I mean now, as in right now, this present moment." I refrained from an adverbial lesson.

"We say 'just now' when it means later. We say 'right now' when it means closer to now than later," explained Karen breezily.

"What the what?" I was sure I must have looked out of my time-oriented mind.

"Just now. Right now. Now now. You need to learn South African time. If I'm coming right now, as in the next five minutes, it means now now. If I'm coming later, I'll say just now. If I'm coming in between right now and now now, I'll say just now. See?"

"Yes."

"Really?"

"No."

From then on I asked for a specific numeric time frame for reference until I learned to tell South African time. The kids caught on quickly. Yesterday, I asked Hudson when his room would be clean.

"Just now," he replied.

THE KIDS not only adopted a nondescript version of telling time, but they learned a colorful vocabulary, thanks to the church.

"What the hell is that damn smell?" came from the lips of a pastor friend one night as she inspected a water leak and damp carpet in the church. I nearly spit out my rooibos tea. I thought perhaps she was having an off night and inwardly commended her for her authenticity.

In the Christian fundamentalist world I grew up in, using the word 'hell' in casual conversation was a clear indication that you had a deviant heart and were probably a registered Democrat.

In South Africa, it was merely a descriptive phrase employed to add punch to an otherwise limp sentence structure. It was what you said when you didn't want to swear.

I listened to an older South African man give a lecture one day. He told a gregarious story, throwing out several 'what the hells' and 'damns' like a progressive California pastor in skinny jeans. Yet, when he repeated something in the story that he found reprehensible, he lowered his voice and bashfully said, "Pardon my French, but that is crap."

The word 'crap' spoken audibly caused him to blush with impropriety. If you visit South Africa, expect to hear 'hells' and 'damns' like it's an adjective modifier. Don't think my kids didn't glom onto this part of their cultural adaptation.

IT'S funny that we all speak English but there are certain words and phrases that just don't translate well. We have four boys and one girl. Our daughter Evangeline is sandwiched between the boys. We tried very hard to keep the language in our house wholesome and above board which lasted until the boys could talk. Ever since they learned to speak, body parts and body fluids became a topic of conversation.

We tried to stifle it, but that only gave it more power. As little kids, they adopted all sorts of euphemisms. I disliked them all. Colloquialisms like 'take a squizz,' 'taking a whizz,' 'going tinkle.' I mean, really, everyone knows what you're referring to, so just say, "I need to find a restroom." I was that mom.

One day, Evangeline and I were at the posh V&A Waterfront, with a new South African friend whom I was just getting to know. Our friendship was so new that I was unsure if she understood my sarcasm, the main method in which I choose to communicate with those I love. Evangeline discreetly whispered that she needed to use the restroom.

"We need to go find a toilet," I said to our friend. "I'm going to look in this building over here. I'll be right back."

"Ok," she replied, "go have a squizz."

"That's funny," Evangeline said. "She's a grown woman and she said 'go have a squizz.'"

I thought it odd myself. I mean, we were well past the potty training stage. But, hey, she had little boys so maybe it' was in her repertoire. After a delightful lunch and local shopping, we prepared to depart ways for the afternoon.

"Thanks for a great afternoon," I said, and set off in separate ways.

"Oh, hey, let's do this again. Give me a tinkle," she yelled across the parking lot.

Sakes alive, what was this woman's deal? Once, sure, maybe. But twice? Was she making fun of my need to use the restroom? Did I use it more often than someone else? For the record, public restrooms are not as readily abundant as in the United States. It makes one skittish.

Later that week, I repeated the odd conversation including my personal commentary to another South African friend who doubled over in laughter. Apparently, "have a squizz" means to have a look around, as in an exploratory expedition. And, "give me a tinkle means" to telephone me. Since our shopping trip, I tinkled several times and I took a squizz all over Cape Town.

✳

SHARK SIRENS ARE REAL. Surfers and swimmers beware. When a Great White shark is spotted, the shark spotters sound the alarm which resembles a tornado siren.

That mom who ran to the edge of the beach and yelled, "SSSSSSWWWWWWWWWIIIIIIMMMMMMMM!!!!" at the top of her lungs to her kids in the ocean? That was me.

BABOON GUARDS ARE REAL. They monitor the neighborhood and answer distress calls from residents. Last Christmas, a baboon troupe raided someone's kitchen, sending hot cross buns flying over rooftops. Baboon guards were called in to chase the troupe back in the wild and out of the suburbs.

THERE ARE other fun phrases you should know before you visit:

Shame. It's a good thing, a bad thing, and a term of endearment depending on your tone and head tilt. Shame is everywhere. "I just had a baby! Oh, shame, look how cute." Or, "I'm late, there's so much traffic. Shame!"

Boot = car trunk

Bonnet = car hood

Robot = traffic light

Biscuit= this is a cookie, not a biscuit. You would never order biscuits and gravy.

Jol = party

Braai = cookout, bbq

Howzit = how are you? "Howzit my bru?"

Izzit = really? Usually used as a question. "I'm going to buy some shoes." "Izzit?"

Boet, bru, brah = brother, mate, dude

Lekker = nice, great, well. "Come, we having a lekker braai."

Bob's Your Uncle = You've got it. "No problem, we grab the boerewors for the braai and Bob's your uncle."

Holding Thumbs = crossing fingers

Touch sides = touching base, checking in. "I just need to touch sides with you to see if you plan to visit South Africa on school holiday? I'm holding thumbs you'll be here soon."

7

Adapt or Die. Or at Least Stop Whining

Travel has a way of stretching the mind. The
stretch comes not from travel's immediate
rewards, the inevitable myriad new sights,
smells and sounds, but with experiencing
firsthand how others do differently what
we believed to be the right and only way.

Ralph Crawshaw

WHEN OUR YOUNGEST BOYS, Ethan and Hudson were
about two years old, we came up with a great plan to renovate
the house. How or why I thought it was a good idea to store a
gallon of paint in their bedroom closet, I don't know. I
thought I replaced the lid tightly and it was tucked away out
of sight.

A good hour and a half into their nap time, I smelled disaster.
The eerie quiet should've piqued my suspicion, but my mother's intuition was greedily soaking in silence and a Diet Coke.

I walked upstairs, panic rising, to a strong smell of latex

paint. There, on the newly carpeted floor sat both blonde-headed boys covered in nothing but Smoky Azurite #9148. They were not the least bit remorseful, after all, the matching cherubs tried to clean up the mess with their clothes from the recently washed and folded basket I left in their room from earlier in the day.

As I told this story to my friend Stella, I said, "Someday I will laugh about this."

She came back with, "If you're going to laugh about it some-day, why not laugh about it now?"

Wise, yet somewhat ludicrous words, you delightful woman, I thought. Why not just get to the point where I can recognize the sheer lunacy of this moment and laugh it off? That's been my life mantra ever since. If it's going to be a funny story later, make it a funny story now. Life is too zesty to be conventional.

This little nugget of advice was probably the best training we could've received for cross-cultural adaptation. Laugh at yourself. Love the lunacy that life brings and relish the utterly unconventional, unpredictable and beautiful wonderment that floats your way.

During that first year, in an effort to shed our American enti-tlement, we learned to say TIA - "This is Africa." I'm aware now that it can be used as a condescending barb, thrown out when things aren't going the way I would have liked, like when I couldn't find any Easter Peeps for Easter. It is like a glorified temper tantrum.

But it could also mean, "Hey, admire that fantastic lady walking down the road with a microwave balanced on her head." Either way, it meant I needed to adapt or go home.

My job was not to create a little America, a home away from home adaptation. Perish the thought! My job was to see this opportunity for the invitation that it was…a chance to peer through the looking glass into a culture, history, and place that had much to teach me.

It was tempting to find other Americans and commiserate and have a little American Christian ghetto which we fortified with our own understanding. That was not why we were here. We were here to discover what we yet do not know. That being said, the first year of unlearning proved to be the most comical.

It took time to adjust to a new normal. Perhaps that was the lesson. One was our normal and now there was a new normal to contend with. There were some things that would never become normal. And some things that would sadden us because they had become our normal and we swore they never would. Just to give you an idea of how differently life operated in the Southern Peninsula of Cape Town, here are a few examples:

Customer service. America, you shut your spoiled mouth if you ever complain about customer service. Here, if it doesn't take you six trips and three weeks to open a bank account, you are living in the lap of luxury.

Thrift stores. I miss thrift stores, garage sales, and legitimate clearance racks. We searched for used furniture initially, but struggled to find anything in our price range. It seemed like either the prices were way too designer-made expensive or there were only wicker and floral lounge suites available. You have no idea how fortunate you are if there's a Goodwill in your town.

Youth sports. Where are the fanatical youth sports programs? Where are the obnoxious parents who routinely get kicked off the sidelines for indecent exposure? Hudson played for a local soccer team. The season was six months long. SIX MONTHS! It was surprisingly cheap compared to what we were paying for travel soccer in the US. And by cheap, I mean $35 for all six months. This included the jersey, which he actually returned after each game so the coach could take them home, wash them and make sure they didn't get stolen, lost or forgotten. The whole "club sport" thing was really, just that, a club.

Speaking of sports, there's no college football. Pause here for a moment of silence. For a diehard Buckeye fan, this is the ultimate sacrifice. There's very little university sporting life to speak of, period. It's like people want to go to college for education or something. I once showed a couple of young South African friends a YouTube clip of the crowd and marching band at an Ohio State football game. They were gobsmacked that these were students their age. I mean, I guess it could be over the top now that you mention it. Good thing I didn't show them a high school football stadium in Texas.

Relationships rule. South Africa is typically a warm culture which means they are highly relational and less individualistic. It's not unheard of to strike up a conversation with a person you've never met. It could be while you're trying on shoes, or perhaps while you're staring at the bags of milk in the grocery store. Where we live, a large population of people do not own cars and the public transportation options are limited, many hitchhike to and from work. It's customary to pick up people in your car and offer a ride.

Upon entering a room it's customary to greet everyone in that room individually. If you don't know someone, you walk up to that person and introduce yourself. You don't eye them suspiciously and then ask your friend for the scoop on the new person, as I would do. Upon leaving that room it's customary to let everyone know individually of your departure so you can wish them well. "Go well. Cheers. Totsiens."

When you email a friend or stranger, it's customary to spend the first paragraph inquiring about the recipient's well-being, day or weather. Should you fire off an email without a proper greeting, or preamble, or *gasp* just use the subject line for efficiency, the relationship, and maybe even your good nature, will come under question.

Relationally, South Africans are typically friendly people except when someone is helping themselves to things like cars, without permission.

Due to the high crime rate, there's a hyper-vigilantism that creates an oxymoron of sorts. People are friendly but also guarded. It's rare to see a front yard without a fence, windows without burglar bars or private security signs not on the house. Light beams, motion detectors, barbed wire or glass shards on the top of fences, spikes along open balconies, and a Neighborhood Watch are pretty standard.

I'm amazed at how quickly we adapted to this and how psychologically traumatizing it is to live like this. I didn't realize the level of paranoia that had seeped into my psyche until we were in rural France and there were no locked doors, no guard dogs and no separation. This level of hyper-vigilance is taxing.

Tea breaks are real. When someone stops by to visit, offer tea. When church is over, offer tea. When there's a gathering with people, offer tea and rusks. Rusks are deceptive by nature. They look like a stale piece of bread dough molded into a little loaf. Turns out, if you eat a whole bunch of little loaves every time you have tea you will gain a healthy amount of weight. Addictive little suckers.

First ladies. The now former president of South Africa, Jacob Zuma, has 6 wives. He is a polygamist who has fathered at least 23 children with 11 women.

Call the baboon hotline. A baboon guard travels with the baboon troop and watches over your neighborhood, defending with a paintball gun against baboons.

Wealth gap. The wealth is not invisible, nor is the poverty. I've never seen so many Ferraris, Porsches, Aston Martins, and Rolls Royces. Yet, the minimum wage for a large population of the working class is less than $1 per hour.

Trading hours. The mall closes at 2 p.m. on Sunday. I will never get used to this. It's not just Sunday hours, but generally, everything closes by 7 p.m. on a good day. Sometimes on a Saturday, shops close at 2 p.m.. Christmas store hours in our mall are SHORTER hours! Shorter! A relational culture trumps a capitalist culture. But wow, is it inconvenient. Hours of operation are called trading hours. Because you trade.

WHAT DO YOU MEAN NO FREE REFILLS?! I am limited to one cup of whatever. One drink! Imagine! I saw a sign once that read, "Free refills. Limit 3."

Car guards. We pay a car guard to watch our car while we are in the mall buying groceries, *not* having a second cup of coffee. Everything is in the mall, including the grocery store.

Utilities to go. We buy electricity when we pay for our groceries. I can also buy pre-paid data and airtime for my phone while I'm buying eggs and bananas. I bring the receipt home, punch the number code into the sub-meter box and voilà! Electricity. It can also run out when no one is paying attention to the level of the meter. We've done that more times than I care to count.

Sometimes we have no electricity because the government turns the entire grid off to help conserve power. Each neighborhood sector takes turns sitting in the dark eating dinner by candlelight.

Utilities are not for everyone. Water, plumbing, and electricity are missing from the homes of millions of people. As I write this, the entire Western Cape province is restricted to 50 liters of water per day per person due to severe drought. A majority of the population has been living without indoor plumbing in their homes. I catch myself complaining about the restrictions and nearly go blind with the privileged truth flashing before me.

The Metric system is a thing. Like most of the known world, South Africa uses the Metric system. Learning to measure solely in grams, liters and meters has become mandatory. I barely remember my fifth-grade math teacher trying to teach us the Metric system because the US was supposedly going to ditch the Imperial system and convert fully to Metric. He seemed just as agitated about teaching it as we were about learning it.

I know that the US technically has a dual system but really, everyone speaks Imperial unless you're buying a drink in a large plastic bottle or running a 5k. In the beginning, I'd go to the deli and the clerk would ask me how many grams of meat and cheese I wanted. I'd stand there like a knob trying to estimate how many grams of shaved ham would feed a family of seven. To avoid embarrassing myself, I'd just ask for a kilogram. Turns out, that's a lot of meat.

I still don't have an exact read on the temperature in Celsius, I just go by feel. If it's going to be 38 degrees on Saturday, it's going to be blasted hot, and 15 degrees means you'll want to wear a coat inside. The speed limit is not 120 *miles* per hour. You only make that mistake once.

Creative traffic laws. There are some hard and fast rules. And there are some rules that function as mere suggestions. Most traffic rules fall into the realm of suggestion. These suggestions invite all manner of creativity and maneuverability. For instance, if the road is closed due to construction, and the detour would be much too far out of your way, then by all means, drive on the shoulder of the opposite lane into oncoming traffic. People will move over for you.

No indoor heating and cooling. We wear coats and jackets indoors during the winter because it's so cold! There is no central heating. When your house is made of brick and cement and the temps outside are 45 degrees Fahrenheit, the inside is c-o-l-d. We all have hot water bottles that we heat up and tuck into our beds to try to stay warm. Often we take them to class or church or anywhere where it might be cold inside. Someone will provide a kettle to heat the water and we will stand in line to either make tea or a hot water bottle and sometimes both.

There are large populations of Cape Town who sleep in one room shacks with a thin barrier between the winter rains and their home. When it's cold and raining I'm cognizant of the truth that just down the road, 20,000 people are watching their homes flood with water as they try to stay warm and dry.

Where's 9-1-1? When our kids were little and old enough to use the phone, we taught them how to call for help. Pick up the phone and dial 9-1-1 and someone will send help, no matter where you are. South Africa has an emergency services phone number and I did try to call it once when someone was getting attacked in front of our house by a mob. The number is 10-1-1-1. When I dialed it, I expected the operator to be tracing my location. Instead, she asked, "What city are you in?" From there a lengthy conversation ensued about which suburb of Cape Town I lived in and where exactly I was located.

Meanwhile, outside in the chaos, I saw my neighbor taking charge. I called the local police before only to be told that the police van was out and when it returned, they would send someone to help. Perhaps this wasn't typical of all of South Africa, but from my experience, there was no guarantee of emergency assistance if I called an emergency hotline.

If we ever move back to the US, we will most likely be bored at the predictability and clock-like management of things like emergency services and driving patterns. If there's not a man pushing a grocery cart full of wood down the middle of the interstate, don't even talk to me about your problem.

8

Dude, Where's My Car?

It's gonna take a lot to take me away from you.
There's nothing that a hundred men or
more could ever do...

TOTO

TO COMMEMORATE our first four months of living in South Africa, we celebrated at the police station. We came home from work in the evening and parked the car in our driveway, not giving it a second thought. Rookie mistake.

There was zero traffic on our road as it was at the top of a hill on a dead-end road. When Kevin opened the front door he expected to walk out, get into the car and drive to the store as he was accustomed to doing. Instead, he stood with the front door wide open and asked me if I had moved the car. He paced around the house as if trying to remember how he misplaced the car the night before while in a completely sober state.

"I think it's been stolen?" Kevin said like he was asking a question on Jeopardy. "I'll take grand theft auto for $400 Alex." Turns out, this was what it felt like to have your car stolen. I only had this feeling once before when I forgot where I parked at the mall.

Suddenly, all of the YouTube comments I had ever read about the safety of South Africa came to life. Yes, cars get stolen here, I had read that. But this car? It's a 25-year old Mazda we rented for $400 a month. This was the real thing. It was not a drill. The car is, in fact, gone. G- O-N-E. Gone.

Granted, it was a rental car. But still, we were newbies and didn't realize that we're not supposed to leave items of value in the car, which was parked in our driveway. Directly in front of our house. At the end of a quiet, dead-end street. Locked.

With no small amount of panic, we realized what valuables we had (stupidly) left in the car. There was this weird feeling like maybe we could negotiate with the car thieves and just ask for a few things of value back if we let them take the car. Funny what becomes important when it's no longer yours.

We left several hoodies and jackets, including Hudson's favorite Columbus Crew hoodie. I mean who in South Africa wants that? (fast forward two years, we saw a dude walking through the grocery store wearing a familiar pair of Columbus Crew soccer shorts). There were soccer balls and one volleyball. Kevin remembered that he put my Canon camera in the boot (trunk) for safekeeping while we were out that day.

Last, but not least, Kevin discovered that his jacket was MIA.

In the missing jacket was his wallet. This wallet contained ALL of our bank cards. Do you see what I'm saying about being novices?

So, not only were we missing money for the month, but our emergency funds were in our US accounts, with access to said funds being the bank cards in the wallet in the pocket of his jacket now long gone. We quickly raced to the computer to log on to our 4 mps speed internet to file a stolen claim with the bank. Once these accounts were canceled we would have to have new cards issued.

But it wasn't like they could just mail them to us. It would be a very long time until those replacement cards ever made it to South Africa.

It's not as if we could waltz into a Bank of America and pick up our new ones. Kinda crazy to think there are no American banks in South Africa. So inconvenient. There was a near hysteria rising up into my throat. In fact, it wasn't staying in my throat. It had pulled up a seat in the kitchen and was making its presence known.

Additionally, we would now have to pay the insurance deductible for the car, which is $400. As if paying more than $400 to rent that car wasn't painful enough! According to the Neighborhood Watch camera surveillance recordings, our car was seen driving down the mountain, away from our house at 7:45 p.m. That was a mere 40-minutes after we got home, which meant we were all home and awake when they stole the car from under our noses.

Literally, the car was stolen while we were inside the house. They could have chosen a BMW or a Mercedes, but no, they chugged all the way up the hill to the very last house and stole a 25-year old Mazda. I don't know why we were singled out, but it kinda felt like this won't be the last time.

9

Hello, Jasmine

"It's the end of the world as I know it, and I
feel fiiiiiiiiiine." Ethan Quist, age 11, upon
being stuffed into a Ford Fiesta. Apologies
to R.E.M.

WHY WAS it so hard to find a rental car that fits our entire
family for less than $800 a month?! Where were the mini-
vans, people? In Ohio, we drove a Dodge Grand Caravan
with dual sliding doors, DVD players and stow-and-go
seating which I sometimes used to smuggle vodka coolers to
soccer tournaments.

Incidentally, we were given that Ohio van as a surprise.
Unbeknownst to us, someone anonymously went to the local
Chrysler dealership and bought it for us and requested that
the dealership deliver it to our house. It was as astounding as
you think. When we moved, we didn't feel it was right to sell
it because it was a gift, so we gave it to another unsuspecting
family.

Back in South Africa, there were no minivans to be found.

Everyone drives a compact car, comparatively. Even cars that claim to be SUV's are small. People, we had just come from the land of the mammoth Ford Excursion and the Hummer SUV. What you were driving was a glorified Ford Escort. Also, why were there so many white and silver-colored cars?

Our second rental car was a purple Ford Fiesta, the 1998 car of the year, or so claimed the bumper sticker. Apparently, it was made to seat four slender people. My people are not slender, not even wispy.

The car rental place gave female names to each of their cars. Ours was 'Jasmine'. We know this because 'Jasmine' was laminated on a large vinyl sticker printed across the back window of our new rental.

Kevin and I sat in front. I tried to adjust my seat as far forward as it would go to accommodate the long teenage legs behind me. Didn't matter, I still rode with someone's knees in my kidneys. Jackson, Dylan, and Evangeline rode in the back seats. The twins rode in the hatchback space.

Oh, did I mention no seat belt law? It's quite all right, we were packed in so tightly, no one had a chance to move a body part. As I was saying, the twins rode in the backspace, legs crossing each other with their faces plastered up against the window while facing backward.

The longest distance we actually drove like this was 45-minutes when we wanted to visit Hillsong Church on the other side of Cape Town. Needless to say, we weren't in a very churchy-mood when we arrived. Correction, the kids weren't in a church-y mood. Kevin and I were fine because we had the most room. When we opened the other doors it was like a can of crescent rolls popping from its package with legs and arms exploding from the vehicle.

We didn't drive Jasmine for more than a few months because she cost us $400 a month and several chiropractor visits. The little financial support we did have dwindled and we had to let Jasmine go. After that, we walked everywhere or took an African taxi, which is a minibus of sorts.

The transportation experience just rose a notch or twelve. Why in the world were cars and petrol (gas) so expensive here? I couldn't see how we would ever be able to afford a car.

10

Fantastic Beasts and Where to Find Them

Avoid eye contact, as baboons may find this
threatening.

Tip from the baboon hotline

WE USED to live in Midwest suburbia and six months later I
was writing about baboons in the kitchen. Did I mention that
the owners of the house we were previously renting (with the
wooden cat family) decided that they wanted to live there
again?

Yes, and apparently it was ok to keep the deposit on the lease
because when we agreed to move out early so they could
move back in, we were breaking the lease. Let's just say that
if I had it to do over again, I'd realize we were being swindled by the owners and the estate agent who negotiated
this deal.

Nevertheless, there we were, homeless with no furniture, not
even a spoon. Because the house we were renting was fully
furnished, we didn't own so much as a utensil. It was Decem-

ber, so summertime was a tough time to look for availability in the Cape, given that it is a tourist destination.

Thankfully, we were housesitting for friends who went to the USA for Christmas. Their house was in Kommetjie, a sweet little surfing village. We got to live in their cute beach house for eight weeks until we found something or until our friends returned. I imagined they would want their house back unless we claimed squatters' rights.

It was a small house with red brick tile and stucco walls and an open floor plan. The kitchen, living room and dining room were all one big space. Three sets of French doors opened to the backyard which was surrounded by a 9-foot tall cement fence.

Thanks to the sheer goodness and generosity of one of our financial supporters, we had some Christmas money to spend on furnishing our future home. We were starting from scratch with the bare necessities. Everyone was getting bed linen and bath towels. That made for a well-received Christmas celebration. We were excited to at least have a few things of our own.

Kevin and I had planned to do a little mattress shopping and since that didn't appeal to any of the kids, they all stayed home. The outside gate was locked for safety reasons. In order for anyone or anything to get into the house, they had to jump over the high fence or climb the roof and jump down into the garden below.

Whichever method that baboon employed, he walked right into the house.

Like a boss.

A friend asked if we had doors and windows here in South Africa. The answer is yes. We don't live in open air huts. However, it was summer and there was no air conditioning. So, we generally kept doors and windows open, to let the breeze and primates in.

Either way, even if the door had been closed, baboons are known to be able to open doors. In fact, I've heard of adult baboons teaching their baby boons to crawl through doggy doors and unlock from the inside of a house. Once the door is opened, the whole troupe comes in. The things one can do with opposable thumbs.

How the kids didn't hear a 200-pound baboon landing with a thud, I didn't know. The bare-butted baboon walked into the house, found the kitchen counter with all my newly purchased fruits and veggies.

Jumped ONTO the counter.

Opened a package of avocados. Peeled the avo. Left the pit.

Ate eggs, left shells.

Opened muesli, was seemingly disappointed with the granola cereal because he shook muesli everywhere.

Opened the peanut butter, stuck his paws in and left a trail in the jar.

Took a bite of butter from the butter tray, then covered it with muesli.

While this was going on, Hudson and Ethan were sitting a mere three feet away, each engrossed in a computer game and a Harry Potter book. Engrossed. NEITHER BOY NOTICED A BABOON IN THE KITCHEN.

Evangeline walked out of her bedroom, saw a fat, furry tail to what she thought was our cat on the counter. Annoyed, she reached for it and realized it was certainly not a cat. It was a baboon. She screamed, ran back to her room, and left her little brothers to fend for their clueless selves.

From inside the bedroom, she yelled for Dylan to come and save them all. Even after all this mayhem, Ethan remained with his back to everything while reading a book. Hudson glanced up just as the baboon landed on the couch NEXT TO HIM with a bag of apples in one hand and a bag of bananas in the other.

Baboons are aggressive when challenged. They have big teeth. This is why there is a neighborhood baboon guard we can call to scare away the baboon. But we did not take notice of such a number and now there was one sitting on the couch.

It was at this moment that Hudson looked up from his electronic device and realized there was a baboon sitting next to him. They made eye contact. The baboon dropped the bananas and sauntered out the open door. He was in no hurry. He parked himself on the back porch where he delightfully ate the apples. The kids grabbed a phone and recorded this activity, through doors which were now closed and locked.

My absolute favorite line of the entire video was, "Mom and dad don't want to come home to a baboon on the porch." So very considerate of them.

When Kevin and I returned from bed shopping, Hudson met us at the door. He inquired about a new bed for the kids. He asked about lunch. No mention of a baboon.

When Kevin saw the kitchen mess, he said, "Who ate like

this?" As if we raised our kids to throw food on the floor and eat directly from the butter dish.

Without any child looking directly at us, deadpan as can be, they all answered, "A baboon." Then they went back to what they were doing as if it was every day they got to drop that news on their unsuspecting parents.

Comedians, all of them.

11

The Rainbow Nation

I have sometimes said in big meetings where
you have black and white together: "Raise
your hands!" Then I have said, "Move
your hands," and I've said, "Look at your
hands" - different colours representing
different people. You are the Rainbow
People of God.

Desmond Tutu

QUESTIONS WE GOT ASKED FREQUENTLY, mostly by
fellow Americans, included, "Are there other white people in
South Africa?" "Is South Africa a country?" "Do you live in a
hut?" "How hot is it there?" and "Do you see tigers?"

People, people, people. The world is small and the Internet is
vast. Africa is not a country. It's a continent made up of 54
recognized countries, give or take. We did not live in a hut.

We lived in a suburb, in a house with cement walls and

running water. We had an amazing view which overlooked False Bay, where Great White sharks congregate. It wasn't cold enough to snow in winter and we only had a handful of days over 90 degrees in summer. The wind was so temperamental that you didn't dare put up an outdoor umbrella. There were no tigers. But there were baboons.

We lived in a smallish suburb 40 minutes outside Cape Town city center. It's called Fish Hoek, which means 'fish corner' in Afrikaans. There are roughly 120,000 residents. If you look at a map of Africa, there is a little peninsula that dangles off the southwestern corner of South Africa. We are on that dangling bit, towards the bottom.

Not only are we near the most southwestern tip of Africa, but as I like to remember it, the furthest I've ever lived from Target. In exchange for commercialism, I'm surrounded by the Indian and the Atlantic Ocean which can be seen on the same day, as they both wrap around us, scattering white sand beaches everywhere. The iconic and majestic Table Mountain rises in the background, surrounded by its bowing subjects of lesser, vineyard-clad mountains and valleys.

You will never see such flora and fauna as in the Western Cape, the land of the beautiful King Protea, the national flower. Here grows a plant kingdom that only graces this area with its presence. Almost 70% of its species are found nowhere else on earth. The Protea family alone will keep your mouth open in awe with its majestic, artichoke-like blooms in different sizes and colors.

Palm trees wave from above while orange, red and purple vines and succulents greet you from below. There are flowers that bloom traditionally in the spring and flowers that prefer the winter months. It is green and lush; surely the garden of Eden left a portion of herself here in South Africa.

On our peninsula, there are basically three routes that lead to the rest of civilization. One road ambles over the mountains that divide us from the rest of Cape Town, while the other two wind around the mountain in opposite directions. Distance-wise, it's not that far, but if you live on this side for any length of time, you begin to bemoan the fact that something requires the drive "over the mountain." We are isolated by a mountain range and surrounded by the seas.

If you drive any further south, you'll land at Cape Point, the home of the Cape of Good Hope. When Portuguese explorer Bartolomeu Dias rounded the cape in 1488, he called it "Cape of Storms" because he sought shelter from a terrifying storm that lasted three weeks. When the storm cleared and he saw the Cape Peninsula clearly, he mapped it out and discovered he was on the rounded tip of Africa.

He planted a cross smack dab on the Cape of Storms and returned to Lisbon with his discovery. To this day, a replica cross still stands. It was his financial sponsor, Henry the Navigator, who renamed it the Cape of Good Hope because it promised a sea route to the riches of Asia. Ten years later, Vasco da Gama would follow this map and open the sea route for the spice trade. The Cape would never be the same again.

The water here reflects the mood of the sky— sometimes bright blue, sometimes green and foamy and other times gray and fuming, void of color and full of sadness. A short drive around the peninsula often turns into whale spotting, detected by the ocean spray or a dorsal fin, or watching a dolphin pod racing to its next destination.

As I said, we don't live in a grass hut. We live in a nice house in a nice neighborhood. The difference though is that South Africa is still reeling from the scars of apartheid which left behind a legacy of poverty and lack of quality education for non-whites. So while I live in a house, not everyone does.

Within a ten minute drive from my house, I will pass a black township where many live in strung together shacks, a colored community with housing projects and an informal settlement nestled in the mountains.

Driving along the southern tip, you come across Scarborough, a crunchy, conservation village that sits on the side of the mountain and sprawls down to the beach. Here, there are regulations to preserve nature, solar panels, rainwater tanks, and organic gardening. Residents make their own kombucha, live in houses overlooking vacant beaches and enjoy some of the purest air in the world.

Continue driving around the winding curve of the mountain and you'll meet a little place called Misty Cliffs, where white water crashes against the rock. The kite surfers love the winds and movie producers love the view. Venture just a few miles farther and you come to the surfing mecca known as Kommetjie (little bowl) where folks walk barefoot down the street and the locals enjoy a morning surf.

The white sand expanse stretches forever while the tide brings in wave after wave of future pro surfers. A lighthouse watches one side of the beach while rows of white Cape Dutch houses with brown thatched roofs sit on the other. Sweet little coffee shops invite you in for fresh fish and chips straight from the fishing boats. There is one primary school where blond-haired kids can be seen playing rugby barefoot on a fenced-in grass field.

Leaving Kommetjie, you'll drive just a mile or two under a series of Baobab trees with skinny trunks and wide heads that look as if they are growing upside down. On the right, you'll come to Ocean View. From the road, you can see block after block of cement buildings, some faded pink and some faded yellow-gray.

Every block looks the same, adorned with freshly washed clothes strung between the flats, hovering over the black asphalt below. Three stories high, and four rows wide, each with a set of cement stairs, the bottom section of some blocks are covered with words, letters and symbols spray-painted in black.

On the corner, a group of young men stand in circle formation with pit bulls on ropes. An elderly lady pushes a baby stroller. A Muslim man passes by, white robe flowing, on his way to the mosque at the top of the street. To the left, there are small homes with wooden bungalows jutting from the back. Spare cars in various stages of repair stand guard at the front door.

The streets narrow and a small girl sits on the sidewalk. A lady stands on the corner talking to her neighbor in a pink bathrobe. A larger than life mural of a baby girl with light brown skin peers down from the building side with a date underneath. She was six months old when she was shot and killed.

Cape Town is a wildly diverse city whose history can better be told through the lyrical storytellers and the living historians. Its European influences are seen, smelled and tasted everywhere. The vineyards speak of French Huguenot ancestry and High Tea reminds me of a proper English habit. The Cape spices and Indian influence can be tasted in the spice of local curry.

I tread lightly on these topics. The small amount of insight that I share here is dwarfed by the depth and width of that which I do not know and have not experienced. I can only ask for grace from my South African friends as I humbly attempt to paint a portrait as vast as yours.

THERE ARE 11 official languages spoken in South Africa, and no, 'African' isn't one of them. Most people speak at least two languages, if not more. We know a man who speaks ten. Ten languages. To be honest, I don't even know if I can count my high school Spanish as one of mine. Here, it's not unheard of for someone to speak to me using English, their fourth language.

Predominate languages we hear in our area of the Western Cape province are Afrikaans, English, and isiXhosa. Afrikaans is a derivative of Dutch. There are lots of guttural sounds. It's also highly descriptive. The word for potato is translated "earth apple." Should you need to know, the word fart is translated "little wind." Gloves are called "hand shoes." I find this infinitely hilarious.

Xhosa is an African tribe second in size to the Zulu. The isiXhosa language is influenced by the Khoi and San languages which uses consonant clicking. Yes, it sounds as spectacular in person as you can imagine.

English speaking South Africans have a delightful lilt that sounds like it could be Australian, but a little more British. It's articulate and clean and ever so lovely to listen to. Their word choice is so proper it makes you sit up straight and order a cup of tea.

Kaleidoscope

SKIN COLORS ARE as diverse as language. You seriously need to read through South Africa's storied history to get even a small idea of the racial history of this nation. Desmond Tutu called it the Rainbow Nation, for good reason. It is complicated and wonderful, but you'll need a documentary and 60 hours to get a grip on it.

With one of the most diverse populations in the world with nearly 60 million people, the categories and population percentages vary, but I'll try to paint a picture from my limited understanding.

A little over 80% of the population self-identifies as black South African, making this the most populous ethnic group in the country according to a recent census. Black South African can refer to Xhosa, Zulu, Tswana, Sotho, Venda or several other tribes of southern Africa. Within each tribe is a language, culture, and history unique to that tribe. The majority of Zulu people live in KwaZulu Natal province. King Shaka was the warrior king who led the Zulu into the annals of history. Former president Jacob Zuma is Zulu.

While the Xhosa people include several different tribes and clans, the group is made up of those who speak isiXhosa as their first language. The heartland of the Xhosa people is the Eastern Cape province, where they make up a large majority of the population — a result of the independent homelands established by the ruling party during apartheid. When apartheid ended, many Xhosa made their way to Cape Town and the Western Cape, where they now make up the vast majority of the black population of Cape Town.[1] Former president Nelson Mandela was Xhosa.

There are multiple other African tribes like Northern Sotho, Tswana, Basotho, Tsonga, Swazi, and Southern Ndebele, but I mentioned Xhosa and Zulu predominately because they are the largest.

THE SOUTH AFRICAN ethnic group known as "coloured" is the largest minority racial group, although they only comprise nine percent of the population. Because the government forced their relocation, there is a large percentage of coloured communities in Cape Town, known as the Cape Coloured.

They speak Afrikaans and English but with a dialect all of their own. I'll never forget the day I was talking to a gentleman on the street who I was struggling to understand. I politely stopped him and apologized, explaining that I can only understand English, deliberately speaking slower and louder. "I am speaking English!" he replied, obviously annoyed. "Oh, sorry," I apologized, mortified that I didn't recognize it.

The multi-ethnic lineage of coloured people comes from parts of Africa, Asia, Europe, and South Pacific islands. I think the coloured community carries some of all of us in their history. They are also some of the most stunningly beautiful people you'll ever see.

Interestingly, the coloured community is called the closest descendants to the indigenous people of South Africa, the Bushman known as the Khoi and San. I get to work with Ishiqua, chief of the Cape Peninsula Khoi. Over a cup of rooibos tea, he will give you a solid lesson in Khoi history, clicking vocabulary and indigenous plants.

During apartheid, coloured people were categorized as such because they were neither black enough to be called black or white enough to be classified white. In a further act of separation, the government designated its own category.[2] This is a painful piece, one that I can barely gloss over without wincing at the amount of trauma that sits between the lines of these sentences.

In America, referring to someone as coloured is not appropriate. In South Africa, it is a distinguishing characteristic of an official people group. The humor, laughter, drama, music and masterful adaptation to life is one of the things I love about the coloured community. If you visit once, you're a welcomed guest. If you return, you're family.

White South Africans comprise roughly 8 percent of the country's population and originate from parts of Europe like Holland, France, and England. The majority of whites are considered Afrikaners, descendants of European settlers from the Netherlands, France, Germany, and Scandinavia.

The Dutch were the earliest and most populous settlers in South Africa, but other groups fleeing religious persecution in France also moved to the country, contributing their influences in the form of good wine.

English South Africans are an even smaller minority. The majority of white South Africans who speak English as their first language claim British ancestry. Britain gained control of the Cape Colony in the 1820s and encouraged immigration.[3]

Though British immigration to South Africa didn't take off until the late 1800s with the gold rush, the small English-speaking minority wields influence in the country.

Indian and other Asian groups are also here. A little granny once informed me that the largest population of Indian people outside of India is found in Durban, South Africa. According to various historical references, Indians first began arriving in South Africa after being imported as indentured work-ers/slaves. At the time, they were labeled as Cape Malays or Cape Coloured, further blurring the distinctions between Indian and coloured during apartheid.

In fact, Mahatma Gandhi spent formative years in KwaZulu-Natal as a young attorney. After being evicted from a first-class compartment on a train, he took up the battle against racial oppression. Some say that key moment began Gandhi's path of peaceful resistance and activism.

Also living here are American foreigners, like us, identified by both volume and swagger, and knee-length basketball shorts. In a country with no NBA, these shimmery culottes are trademark American attire.

I'm often accused of "swallowing my words," making it hard to understand my American accent with our nasal tone which sounds like I have a "blocked up nose."

These shallow descriptions don't begin to scratch the surface of the beauty here. There really is no classification or label that can describe the magnitude of what it means to be South African.

This was a stark contrast to my mostly homogenous upbringing with monochromatic language and skin tone. This was much, much richer and answered the longing of my heart to know myself outside of myself.

1. www.sahistory.org.za/article/homelands
2. www.en.wikipedia.org/wiki/Coloureds
3. www.sahistory.org.za/article/britain-takes-control-cape

12

I Can Say Desmond

Masiphumelele: [mahsee poom a lay lay] an
isiXhosa phrase meaning "we shall
succeed"

WHEN I WAS IN COLLEGE, I remember staring at magazine photos (because the Internet wasn't a thing) of places in South Africa where people lived in cardboard shacks and makeshift homes with no running water. It was the early 1990s and South Africa had made its way onto the global stage in a swirl of controversy and protest.

I swore to myself that someday I would see these communities in real life. Fast forward 20 plus years and I was standing inside one of those iconic magazine photos which hadn't changed since the first day I peered in through glossy paper.

We joined a locally run non-profit organization who worked in several "informal settlements," "shantytowns," "communities" or "townships." We started our South African education in Masiphumelele, a black community formally known as Site 5. Here's a bit of local history:

In the early 1980s, a group of 400-500 black people started the first informal settlement close to where Masiphumelele is today - in the bushes around that area where today the huge Longbeach shopping mall is located.

Under Apartheid laws these families were repeatedly chased away by force. Later they were told that this area was for black people only to work, but they had to live in the poorly set up township of Khayelitsha, more than 30 kilometers away.

Those who had found some work in the Fish Hoek area tried, again and again, to move back to their former homes.

Only after Apartheid had ended a group of people from Khayelitsha, joined by a few thousand people from the Eastern Cape who hoped to find work in the Western Cape, started again in 1991/92 to set up their own community at the area which was then known as "Site 5," but was renamed Masiphumelele by the people soon after.1

Most of the residents are Xhosa, some are African foreigners from Zimbabwe, Mozambique, Somalia, Malawi, and the DRC.

The main entrance and exit boast a sign that reads "Masiphumele" in broken tiles and mosaics. It's an isiXhosa word meaning 'we shall succeed.'

From the entrance, it doesn't appear to be a place of significant size as you can only see a few storefronts with spray-painted business logos and a taxi rank with large vans sitting in front. The taxis are the main form of transportation, other than feet.

Makeshift fruit and vegetable stands slope into the vacant

land in front of the entrance and the sidewalk is covered with piles of clothing for sale from the individual entrepreneurs standing beside them. Scores of people walk the sidewalks and streets between the shopping mall and Masi.

There are a few brick and mortar houses but mostly shacks have been built on whatever piece of open land was available or open for rent, including wetlands that flood terribly when it rains. Rows of portable toilets line the street in groups of eight or so because for the majority, indoor flushing toilets are an exception.

Lines of electrical wires crawl down a single electrical pole like spider legs, attaching to different shacks next to the satellite dishes on the roof.

Colorful, corrugated tin and cardboard pieces are patched together like a mismatched quilt to represent a single room house. A hot plate or countertop stove, an electric kettle and possibly a small refrigerator make up the kitchen which is the bedroom which is the living room. During heavy rains, water pours in through the roof, through gaps in the aluminum walls and rises up from the saturated soil below.

Neighbors live within inches of each other. Small fires dot the side streets, cooking *nyama*, the delicious smell of roasted meat fills the air. Chickens strut across your path as if to ask why you are there. Stray dogs meander, dodging rocks thrown by little boys wearing shirts that show their round, brown tummies peeking out, giggling.

Upon entering Masi, I instinctually understood that I, an *Umlungu*, didn't automatically have a space here. There was an existing fabric of belonging that superseded the physical context. There was a tribal family, a community, a family, a powerful and rich history. However, once accepted by the community, I understood the gift of this acceptance.

My heart was saddened and I was overwhelmed at the indignity of those having to use an outdoor community toilet or having no running water, walking in the rain to work, largely recognized only for gardening or domestic help. Unhygienic living conditions have led to a healthcare crisis. Differing organizations estimate that a significant percentage of the community are infected with HIV and/or TB. 2

We were introduced to Masi through the eyes of the Xhosa young people we worked with whose names I struggled to pronounce. The language, isiXhosa, liked to join consonants together in configurations that my American tongue was not fit to articulate. Many names had clicking consonants instead of phonetic sounds. People were kind and gracious at my attempt to pronounce their names.

I enthusiastically attempted Ntandazo's name when I first met him. I was so confident that I had it right I marched right up to him and said, "You must be Dondazal!" I swore he flinched.

He smiled at me, nodded his head hesitantly, eyes pleading for someone to help him escape the crazy, white lady. Names like Ntandazo, Noxolo, Nandipha, Sondizwa, and Desmond became more than names, they are friends we love. (Side note: I could pronounce Desmond straight away).

The exciting learning stages were fun and challenging and filled with naiveté. What I did not yet know was that places like Masi were the birthplaces of youth uprisings and acts of resistance that would bring down the remnants of a racist regime and restore a nation.

But at that moment, my pity only served to increase indignity when I came in the name of charity instead of justice. But that lesson will be learned soon enough.

1 www.hokisa.co.za/historyofmasiphumelele

2 "Living Hope Masi Page". Living Hope. Archived from the original on 16 January 2012. Retrieved 4 December 2011.

13

Who Invited Awkward White Girl?

May the Angel of Wildness disturb the places
Where your life is domesticated and safe,
Take you to the territories of true otherness
Where all that is awkward in you, Can fall into
   its own rhythm.

John O'Donohue

SHE SAID "TRADITIONAL DRESS." To me, "traditional dress" for a bridal shower on a hot, summer Saturday afternoon, meant a cotton skirt and flip flops. To her, it meant African traditional dress complete with celebratory face paint. Noting the difference of interpretation, I already sensed with some apprehension that I was clearly underdressed.

We met on a narrow side street in Masiphumelele, in a one-roomed church building. Yellow and blue balloons hung from the ceiling and soft tulle was tied around the backs of plastic chairs. A small table was set with refreshments, namely Cheetos and marshmallows.

The bridal shower was scheduled to begin at 2:30 p.m. Knowing that time was but a suggestion, I arrived at 3:15 p.m. There were a few ladies present, none of whom I knew. I was only there in the supporting role cast. A friend of mine, Sondy, was the emcee and invited me along.

It was my first Xhosa bridal shower called *amabhaso*. I spoke very little isiXhosa. I could ask for the toilet, say my name and exchange a few pleasantries. After about 30 seconds, my conversational isiXhosa was over.

At 4 p.m. more women, a pastor's wife and the bride-to-be arrived. I never actually caught the name of the pastor's wife, only the title. If the women weren't dressed in African traditional dress, they were dressed like guests of honor at a royal wedding. Sunday-best dresses, high heels, necklaces with matching earrings and clanging bracelets. We began with singing. There was always singing. No music, no instruments, just voices that sounded like the Brooklyn Tabernacle Choir.

They didn't sing in English and I struggled to keep up with their rhythm. Namely, they had it; I didn't. The pastor's wife was wearing an emerald, iridescent dress with gold high heeled sandals. The dress had ruffles that sparkled like waves. She shimmered like an ocean current while she spoke about the importance of marriage. The young bride-to-be, called an *umakoti*, sat at a special table in the front of the room. She fidgeted but smiled at the pastor's wife.

I didn't see a gift table, so I kept my card in my purse. We sang for about an hour. One very long hour. The refreshments were passed around. I took a marshmallow. I never turn down a marshmallow. As the singing ended, I wondered if this was the end of the shower. Maybe it was not traditional to give gifts. But I was ever so wrong.

As I was happily munching, a slender lady wearing a sleeveless coral dress seated by me suddenly burst into song. She could have been a Grammy contender. As she was singing, she stood, picked up a gift bag hidden beneath her seat and made her way to the front of the room. Once in the open space, she proceeded to dance and sing. When she finished, she presented her gift bag, then gave a 10-minute speech to the bride.

I thought this was perhaps a special presentation, a guest-of-honor or something. Then, to my left, another lady belted out a song. She sounded like Aretha Franklin. She sang, rose, walked to the front of the room, spun and sashayed in her dress and presented her gift, followed by her speech.

The pattern repeated itself. Sing, dance, speech, gift. I realized with a fair amount of horror, that if I was going to present my gift, I would have to sing, dance and give a speech.

FOR THE LOVE OF ALL THAT WAS GOOD AND PURE.

If only I could sing, dance, speak isiXhosa or heck, I'd have settled for knowing the bride. There is something that African mamas teach their children before they are born. I don't know how they do it, but they emerge from the womb innately knowing how to sing and dance. It's in their African blood; a gift of the land. It's decidedly not in mine.

Heck, when Jackson was a baby, as a new mom, I remember trying to sing him to sleep. The more I sang, the more he cried. When I stopped singing, he stopped crying.

Nearly two hours later, I was thinking that I would slip out the door, unnoticed. Suddenly, my friend the emcee, with a microphone in hand, was standing at the front, speaking to the ladies, making a copious amount of direct eye contact with me. I grew both suspicious and uneasy.

She then translated to English: "Cristi, will you come up here and say a few words about marriage?" SWEET SASSY. Let the ground swallow me up or at the very least, let me find the marshmallows and stuff them into my mouth to render my speech useless. What was I going to say to a group of women I didn't know, in a language I didn't speak, in a culture not my own? I started to itch. I have the hives.

I was sure right then that the bride was looking at me wondering, "Who invited awkward white girl?" So I bartered and pleaded with God to give me something to say in the three seconds remaining until I had to take that microphone.

"Don't worry," said Sondy. "If you speak, you don't have to sing. I know you people don't do that." I had never been so thrilled to be lumped into the "you people" category.

It was then that I realized what an honor it was to be standing here, at this celebration. How often did I make the effort, on a Saturday afternoon to get dressed in my finest clothes, actually spend time doing my hair, *and* put on my high heels?

When was the last time I saw this kind of gathering as a reason to celebrate the beauty of time, the passage from girl to woman, from milestone to milestone?

When was the last time I sang so loudly that the melody carried out onto the street? When was the last time I let myself twirl and dance in an open space to celebrate with abandon the life of another woman? There is something universally beautiful when women celebrate each other. These women gave me the gift of a mirror on that

Saturday afternoon– a mirror so I could see what celebration looked like and how I had lived a life reserved.

I always restrained myself out of a sense of propriety at the very moments in life when I should have celebrated with abandon. What is life if not to be celebrated? What was a celebration without a song and dance? These women knew a depth of living that my cautious and controlled life could only watch from a distance.

Here, behind the homes built of tin and cardboard, these women gave gifts that matched the occasion, not their economic status. The silk of a new scarf, the smell of new leather, the surprise and delight of a new bride as she begins to unwrap her new life.

Here, where toilets don't flush and faucets don't flow, and where the future is temporary, this event was worthy of time. Each moment was felt, seen, heard, tasted. Nothing was wasted, especially not moments like these.

This bridal shower began as a gift to a young bride and closed with a gift to me.

14

Paradise Lost

Every being cries out in silence to be read
   differently. Do not be indifferent to these
   cries.

Simone Weil

*A TEENAGE BOY was stabbed to death in Masiphumelele on
New Year's Eve-by other teenage boys. Shortly after
midnight, a fight broke out.*

Uninterrupted blue sky, calm ocean waves, mountains
reflecting in the vast water; summer is stunning in South
Africa. White sand, palm trees, vibrant flowers in bloom.
Post-card perfect.

*News of the murder didn't make it into the newspaper. No
outcry. No headline. No mention. Not a ripple. We knew him,
the boy. He had been to the teens club with Kevin. We even
knew of the boys that killed him: 12, 13, 14-year olds.*

It was a Southern Hemisphere summer. Holidays. Sun-tanned

tourists and families on holiday filled the beaches and shops. Bermuda shorts and sunglasses and drinks with umbrellas lazed down the boardwalk while the water and laughter sparkled in the background.

One of Hudson's 14-year old soccer teammates was raped and murdered last week in his home in Masi. One of the greatest lies ever perpetuated is that some lives aren't worth as much as others. This is evil at its best. Disguised in paradise. This was one of those tragedies we never wanted to have to explain to our kids. But we did. Now, the community turned to mob justice which looked like suspects being stoned and burned to death; necklaced with rubber tires set alight, forced around the shoulders of men.

The terrifying thought that went through my mind was dear God, his mother. How would she survive this? I didn't know what we would've done in the USA had this happened, but it seemed like here, we paused briefly and continued. There was no talk of counselors or carry-in dinners for the family.

As tragedies do, it passed on the face of the calendar and so too, it passed through the valley and then out again.

Another day, another life.

15

Sondy's New Baby

Tread softly! All the earth is holy ground.
It may be, could we look with seeing eyes.
This spot we stand on is a paradise!

Christina Rossetti

I LEFT her house wishing I had what she had, knowing it was much too late for me. We drove through the crowded, make-shift road, the smell of chicken pot pie and sugar cookies filling the car. We drove around uneven potholes, stray, loping dogs, strutting chickens and kids playing soccer in the streets.

We walked underneath the clothesline, soaking with freshly washed bedding. We walked around the government installed outhouses lined in a row, wooden, painted with green doors. We walked over stones and uneven ground, flesh-colored, grainy sand mixed with dirt and gravel. A metal door opened to greet us, inviting us inside. We wiped our feet on a rose-patterned floor mat.

My friend, Sondy, and her husband were on day six with their newborn son. She was glowing and lovely and sat folding clothes, fresh from the clothesline. I couldn't fathom hanging laundry after a C-section. I was barely coherent.

Her house was a single room, barely larger than my kitchen. There was one bed and one TV. One room. The new parents sat on the bed while we stood in the kitchen/living room/doorway.

The sun shone through behind her, casting happy rays on her new family. I held their beautiful newborn baby boy, with huge brown eyes and black curly hair - a sweet new baby smell, round, brown cheeks, wrapped in a bundle, eyes fluttered open and lips made sucking noises.

Then it hit me. There was no bathroom. The bathtub bucket hung on the wall when not in use. There were no sinks or toilets. There was no running water, which made the gift that I brought to this precious new mom totally inappropriate.

I stared at my gift bag in dismay. It was too late to hide it, with its billowing tissue paper erupting from the top of the gift bag, demanding to be seen. Just like a toy jack-in-the-box, it began as a good idea but when it was opened, it brought nothing but heart palpitations and an anxiety attack.

Sondy graciously opened my gift of organic, lemongrass-infused, all-natural bubble bath and body wash and ignored my cluelessness. I inwardly cringed with embarrassment. It was a good thing Evangeline baked Sondy's favorite sugar cookies which partially made up for my thoughtlessness.

Each time my kids came into this world, church ladies brought casseroles and relatives sent Hallmark cards filled with crisp, new $20 bills. My mother came to tackle the embarrassing laundry and cleaned the house.

New moms get pampered and celebrated. Gifts and flowers and balloons fill the house. New babies have their own sweet bassinets and new baby powder soft smell. Sterile, clean, new.

New babies weren't meant to live in a house made of tin, wood, and cardboard on unstable ground. When it rains and floods, everything is soaked and the wind howls and the roof caves and the frigid rain pours into cracks and soaks the family bed.

This arrested my entitlement. I admired this bravery, this determination. If I lived here, would I be a mother, would I attempt to raise a family? I mean, when Mary gave birth to Jesus, there was no maternity ward, just a manger. It begged the question–what was I made of? Was I brave enough to battle the weather, the neighbors, the poverty, the violence, and raise a child? She and her African sisters and mothers were made of steel where I was made of cotton.

My friend was gracious to excuse my softness, my neediness, my Western world expectations. She knew I could not do what she was doing. She knew I couldn't handle her world. And she loved me anyway. She invited me into her world. We gradually learned from each other. She came into my world, and I stepped gingerly into hers.

The more time I spent in her world, the more I understood the proverb, "She walks in strength and dignity." She walked like I never could, nor will be asked to walk. She walked, back straight, head high, new life swaddled on her back. She is a proud mother. And I and am proud to be her friend.

16

Hamba Kahle, Tata Madiba

People must learn to hate, and if they can learn
to hate, they can be taught to love, for love
comes more naturally to the human heart
than its opposite.

Nelson Rolihlahla Mandela

I MADE A WILDLY popular decision to cancel the family's
Sunday afternoon surfing plans, opting instead for a family
trip downtown for a history lesson. My kids loved weekend
history lessons as much as they loved spontaneous museum
stops en route to our family vacations.

In my defense, the last stop was the Carl Sandburg museum I
discovered on our road trip to Disney World. I saw the sign
advertising it and there was just no good reason to pass a
poet's house without spending a few hours in devoted admiration. Besides, there was just no competition between one of
America's greatest poets and a giant mouse with no pants.

News of Nelson Mandela's death on December 5, 2013, spread

quickly. The minute it was announced, all flags hung at half-staff and bittersweet songs began playing on national radio interspersed with Mandela's own voice from his famous speeches.

His picture hung in storefronts, on bridge overpasses, on skyscrapers. It was even spotlighted with laser lights on Table Mountain, one of the newest seven natural wonders of the world.

The smaller stores had chalkboard signs on easels sitting out front, where normally they advertised daily specials. Now they shared loving sentiments. "Sweet sleep Tata," "We love you forever, RIP Madiba" and the Zulu phrase meaning to go well, "Hamba kahle, Madiba."

We spent this particular Sunday downtown in front of Cape Town City Hall, the sight of Nelson Mandela's first speech as a free man. Standing on an ornate balcony, straight from prison, he gave a speech to 50,000 people who gathered to see the man who was the face of the anti-apartheid movement-a face that hadn't been seen for 27 years.

Now, I was standing in front of the same building, 23 years later, reading notes and admiring bursts of color in floral bouquets left by the very people he fought to free. A large crowd gathered, huddled in select circles.

A small child was perched high on a man's shoulders, while her chubby hands grasped a miniature South African flag. *Nkosi sikelel' iAfrika was* playing on repeat from an impromptu band below.

The city seemed calm. It felt unified like it was taking a deep breath before the exhale. Despite driving down Nelson Mandela Boulevard, seeing Mandela's face on escalators, collectible coins, storefronts, oil paintings, and t-shirts, nothing could have prepared me for this. This country was showing the world just how much Africa's son meant to them, regardless of political affiliation.

Growing up in America, nestled in the hand of conservative politics, I knew enough to know that while every president had his fans, there was an equal and opposite reaction to his popularity, which subsequently could be found on the competitive news network.

But here, I could see that something was different, especially when the Premier of the Western Cape, the ANC's main political opposition, changed her Twitter profile picture to one of Nelson Mandela.

My family was witnessing the country's mourning and celebration of this iconic man, well aware that it was not every day we got to celebrate the life of a legacy. In fact, never in my life had I shared a space where one man brought together a nation that once bowed and strained under strict apartheid policies and human indignity.

That here, Zulu, Xhosa, Indian, white, and coloured were standing together is a testament. I knew there were those in this crowd who were young enough to remember his legacy and old enough to remember the horror.

After the National Party gained power in 1948, its all-white government immediately began enforcing existing policies of racial segregation under a system of legislation called apartheid. Apartheid, in Afrikaans, means apartness or separateness, literals "apart hate."

This lasted until 1990. During this time, Mandela was a key

player, driving the anti-apartheid movement and was famously jailed for 27 years as a result.

Growing up in America's heartland, I first heard Nelson Mandela's name mentioned with the description "jailed black terrorist" preceding it. South African media used the same descriptor since their news was filtered by the National Party, who censored and controlled what the general population was permitted to see. Turns out, my conservative American vocabulary was an echo of the apartheid government's voice.

Now, we were remembering the life of this incredible man who was a political prisoner for almost three decades and then was voted into the presidency four years later as South Africa's first black, multi-racially elected president. Amongst incredible diversity of culture and language, following the harshest of governments, Mandela stepped into what most expected to be a civil war. Instead, Africa's only bloodless revolution unfolded.

Considering his past and the propaganda surrounding his persona, it was not surprising that many expected South Africa to launch into a bloody civil war after Mandela's release. Tensions were high, matters were unsure. His stance was unexpected. "As I walked out the door toward the gate that would lead to my freedom, I knew if I didn't leave my bitterness and hatred behind, I'd still be in prison," he said.

MY FRIEND JOHAN gave a great summary from his perspective as an Afrikaner:

It is foreign to call him a terrorist. I was seven-years-old when Madiba [Nelson Mandela] was elected president. I suppose the nagging question at the back of the mind of the doubters is, can a leopard change his spots? The answer is yes - his spots and a nation.

Madiba was not God. He was a man, with failings and failures. Before his incarceration [some] called him a terrorist. In context, considering the oppression he and millions of other black Africans endured, one might justify his actions. These types of actions are not uncommon. The world over, throughout history, people have responded the same way when oppressed.

What is significant about Madiba is the change in him. During his incarceration, he followed an entirely different strategy. This is proven, not in whole but in part, by him learning Afrikaans. Madiba then studied Afrikaner history in Afrikaans. He wanted to understand his oppressor, not to defeat him in an Ender's-game-like way, but through forgiveness and love.

What was most telling to me (from my outsider's observation), was the expression of deep love and adoration the people of this nation had for their president. It mattered not the skin color, religion, culture, or language, there was a palpable appreciation, an intimate knowledge of their leader. He was lovingly called Tata Madiba, their 'father.'

It was not hard to see and feel that this nation's children

revered him. There was an unspoken understanding, a connection between Madiba and his children. They knew him, and they had journeyed a long walk to freedom together.

To try to understand it seemed too arrogant, so we observed it from the outside.

Nelson Mandela's funeral was held on Sunday in his home-town in the Eastern Cape province, a long way from Cape Town. Nevertheless, all the grocery stores and our local shop-ping mall remained closed out of respect. Never mind that it was a mere two weeks before Christmas, when, undoubtedly, a large profit could be made.

This was a nation in mourning. Mandela's memorial service drew 90 heads of state from all over the world. Presidents and kings and prime ministers from Iran, Cuba, Israel and the United States shared a stage on the televised service broad-cast worldwide. Bono was here, as was Prince Charles. This was no ordinary president.

MY FRIEND NATASHA told the story of meeting Mandela in person. She said as a little girl she remembered him walking right up to her, and bending down said, "Little girl, if you want to, you can be president of South Africa someday too."

A lot of people have met Nelson Mandela, and he treated everyone as equally important. "I knew, that when he put on that Springbok jersey, which was the epitome of the apartheid government, that this was no ordinary man. Even the most racist people had mad respect for what Mandela taught our country," said one of my rugby-playing friends.

That we, as Americans, got a front-row seat to witness the outpouring, the reverence, the appreciation, and admiration, was beyond humbling. It felt like an intensely private moment but one South Africa was willing to share with us, and the world.

17

Private Eyes Are Watching You

A strong woman stands up for herself.
A stronger woman stands up for everybody
   else.

Source unknown

OUR DRUG DEALING neighbors were finally evicted after nearly nine months of court dates, police raids and sleepless nights. In one single house located outrageously close to ours, lived the suburbs' most notorious BIG's. Several convicted murderers, drug dealers, and run-of-the-mill-thieves had taken up residence in a three-bedroom house with a lovely garden.

It was hard to say just how many people lived there. Someone lived in the broken down van parked out front with a yellow, sun-faded bedsheet covering the window. Some lived in the backyard, making bedding from twigs and leaves. They kept odd hours and did not keep their voices down.

The driving force behind their eviction was my neighbor,

Bing Crosby. She ruled the neighborhood dressed in a golf polo and khaki shorts. She was the Chuck Norris of the southern peninsula.

Meeting Bing was one of the delightful gifts that Cape Town gave us. She looked after our kids, pets and the house. Not only did she operate a sanctuary for rescued tortoises, but she also operated on our kids, seeing that she was a surgical nurse, or 'sister' as they are called in South Africa.

One time while surfing, Jackson had an unfortunate rendezvous with a fiberglass surfboard fin. It sliced the bottom of his foot clean open. Because she was always prepared for emergencies, Bing was there in an instant to clean the wound and much to our surprise, whipped out a surgical stapler and proceeded to sample the bottom of Jackson's foot back together. The only thing she didn't have was pain killers.

According to Bing, she moved from Scotland as a little girl and grew up in Rhodesia (now called Zimbabwe) during the Bush War, also known as the Zimbabwean War of Liberation in the country just north of South Africa.

Despite standing about 5'5, she carried herself with a fearless authority. If you told Bing that she couldn't do something, her reply would most likely be, "Yes, I bloody well can." I once saw her painting her rain gutter while standing on a step ladder which was perched on a kitchen chair. When she hits 70-years-old in a few years, maybe she will slow down a bit. Likely not.

Combined with her tenacious exterior was a cheeky personality and love for cruise ships, particularly Disney cruises. Bing often paired her signature khaki shorts with a souvenir shirt from her latest cruise and a pair of neon green, yet sensible Crocs.

Her dark blonde hair was cropped short, with only a few gray hairs sprinkled throughout. She rarely wore make-up and had a natural beauty, a mischievous twinkle in her eye and, when she chose to bestow it, a contagious smile.

Our houses were separated by a low wall behind the main security gates. When Bing wanted to visit, she spryly hopped the fence and gave me a warning whistle before calling, "Hey Crissy!"

Every year for Christmas she gave our family a box of 150 different kinds of shortbread biscuits (cookies). There was really no shortbread differentiation, in my amateur opinion, just different shapes of the same cookie.

When we left the house, Bing carefully monitored it for us. We knew exactly who lived in the area and who didn't. In the southern peninsula, I could pretty much guess where someone lived based on the color of their skin. I was told that if I were to visit other parts of South Africa, like Johannesburg, I would not see the same segregated demographic. But here, we mostly live separated from each other. Black, coloured and white typically live in distinct areas, as if history's demarcation still holds true.

Strangely, we didn't really talk to our neighbors much. With the exception of a few friendly faces, most people came home from work, drove through their security gate and locked the door behind them for the night.

The house three doors down from us had a cement fortress of a wall that surrounded the perimeter. Violet bougainvilleas wound up the sides, softening the monstrous divide. Three

Rottweilers guarded the castle as they snarled and hovered over the 15-foot wall. I don't generally do cardio in public but I would go from a casual stroll to full sprint just to get past that house.

The Neighborhood Watch association was a cult unto its own. Mind you, it was not without reason or merit. In small-town Ohio, the Neighborhood Watch consisted of two elderly ladies who peeped out the window with a menacing glare. It meant people trading house keys with one another while on vacation. Cape Town takes Neighborhood Watch to a level somewhere between private investigators and Jason Bourne.

I GOT to listen to a light-hearted conversation between Bing and another Neighborhood Watch veteran named Stacy. Stacy is a 50-something petite, blonde who was wearing a lemon yellow shirt with small whale print, white capri pants, and practical shoes. She was formidable.

Stacy: "I walked to Kalk Bay last night to see if I could find the muggers who got the lady down the street. I was wearing all black, a balaclava (handkerchief) over my face so just my eyes showed and my bulletproof vest. Those boogers still recognized me. I walked by them and they said, 'Hi Stacy'."

Me: "What are you doing now?" Stacy was leaning over the ledge of Bing's balcony staring at a conversation taking place below us on the street.

Stacy: "I'm recording the scene. These sunglasses I'm wearing are recording everything."

Bing: "Stacy, do you remember when you went on that sting

because that one street was getting hit with car thefts? You hid in your car, waiting. Sure enough, the criminals showed up and tried to steal a bakkie (truck). While they were busy breaking into the truck, you got out of your car and chained their axle to the car undercarriage. When they tried to get into their car to run away, they were stuck. Then you chased them down the street."

Stacy: "Yes, I remember." At this point, Stacy paused to take a radio call for help that came in on the Neighborhood Watch radio. False alarm. The cameras that scan the roads did a nice job of recording all kinds of movement, who came and went on the road.

Stacy: "It's the court systems. We got a call one night about a badly injured man on his back steps. We arrived only in time to watch him die right there. The thieves, two men, and a woman, just now are going to trial. This was in 2011. She turned state's evidence. He got 10 years. 10 years. For murder. And that's a good sentence."

Bing: "There was the one time there were some bin pickers digging through rubbish late at night. They weren't supposed to be here at that time so I pulled over to tell them to go home. They told me to booger off in Afrikaans. I had two broken arms at the time or I would have tackled them."

Stacy: "Bing can hold her own. Usually, when we call the police, they send Bing in first and offer to back her up." They both laughed at this.

Bing: "I don't fear the criminals. I was trained up in Rhodesia in the Bush War."

Stacy had to leave at that point, but not without peering through a pair of binoculars at a group up on the far mountain smoking marijuana behind a rock. She called it into that area's Neighborhood Watch who promptly adjusted their surveillance cameras to scan the area. They probably had a heat-activated movement detection system that was scanning pupils right then.

The bottom line is this: You don't mess with a Neighborhood Watch. Do.Not.Mess.

18

Pollsmoor Prison

Compassion isn't just about feeling the pain of
others; it's about bringing them in toward
yourself. If we love what God loves, then,
in compassion, margins get erased. 'Be
compassionate as God is compassionate,'
means the dismantling of barriers that
exclude.

Gregory Boyle

I ASSUMED my tears were initially triggered by the sight of
arms and hands reaching through the jail bars. When I got my
emotions under control, I realized it was not the sheer horror
of the scene that caused my tears, but the tangible presence of
the conflict.

Kevin and I visited South Africa's notorious Pollsmoor Prison
for a "prayer walk" after normal visiting hours. Pollsmoor is
one of South Africa's maximum-security prisons which once

housed Nelson Mandela in the latter part of his prison sentence. The guards (called warders) volunteered to work off duty for no pay, just to escort us from block to block.

We met about 85 other people from various Cape Town churches on a late Thursday evening. This is locally known as a "prayer walk." There was no agenda except to voluntarily spend time inside the prison itself, instigating an energetic disruption in the form of prayer.

We gathered in a small room for a time of worship and rule explanations. Our group was an eclectic bunch, from the college students in North Face coats to shriveled, toothless women wearing layers of assorted material and head wraps.

Former prisoners now living this side of grace rubbed shoulders with a 300-pound rugby player who was leading us in songs, and here we were: a typical American couple, staring wide-eyed at the colorful mix of people who ventured into prison on a chilly weekday night.

The not-so-large room filled with guitars, tambourines, maracas, a saxophone, and even an accordion. Let me tell you a little something about what I've observed about coloured and black folks when they worship: They sing. Loudly. They dance and move and bring life to every passionate word. Every verb requires physical action.

One collective voice lifted high the name of Jesus, the Liberator, from inside that room, echoing off the cement walls and bouncing around the cold metal. If there was anyone sleeping, they were surely awake now.

The cold air of the prison began to warm. People removed layers of winter clothes. The passionate prayer required energy and kinetic motion. The presence of light filled the room. Then they led us into the darkness.

It was here that I couldn't hold back shocking, visceral tears. There were no words to describe the rage that arose within me. In place of words, the salty tears were the only expression of anguish I had-an expression I could not contain.

A uniformed warder led us through a urine and bloodstained labyrinth until we were dumped into an outdoor courtyard, surrounded by two floors of prisoners, looked down at us from inside.

From where we stood, we could look into the clearly illuminated night sky. The stars competed along with the barbed wire encased buildings for our visual attention. From where the prisoners stood, they could see us.

A yellow spotlight flickered on and off as all 85 of us walked into the open space that began to suffocate me, despite the open-air courtyard. The prisoners surround us on all sides, in different tiers, two stories high.

This was cell block D, men's maximum security. Prison uniforms hung outside the windows, tied in knots from the steel bars. Behind us, the heavy doors slammed and locked. We were all prisoners now.

The outside light dimmed and the yelling began. Unintelligible phrases filled the silence; a cacophony of condescension and whistling. Used condom wrappers, trash, and bits of who knows what floated down from the second level. We separated and covered every inch of the courtyard.

We began to pray. We walked around, arms uplifted, some audible proclamations, some silently determined. Ten, fifteen minutes passed. The yelling quieted. Arms lunged at us from between the bars, pleading arms. Come over here. Pray for me. Hands waved to get attention. *Are you praying? Pray for me.* A dark corner whispered amen.

Then it began, in the corner of the second tier. A recognizable melody. From the inside. It was one of the songs we sang earlier that evening. A hymn called 'Bless His Name.' Arms outstretched from inside the cell, a medley of male voices sang into the courtyard. The prisoners were singing back to us.

Next to the little old lady with no teeth and the 300-pound rugby player, there was a claim. A stake. Darkness would not rule. There was a battle for love. Here, in the land of the hurting and the hurtful, there was hope. Hope that began with love. And continued with love. And it will end with love.

The atrocities surfaced and seethed. The prison was unrelenting. There was a clamoring for hope. There were hallelujahs in the darkness.

19

Our Boys Are in Prison

A procession of angels pass before each
person, and the heralds go before them,
saying, "Make way for the image of God!"

Midrash *Deuteronomy Rabbah,* 4:4

I DIDN'T SLEEP WELL. The stench remained in my nostrils
so every time I inhaled, I could smell where I'd been. It
reminded me of the times I used to serve dinner to homeless
folks in Columbus with my friends Mim and Liz. The odors
soaked into my clothes so I came home smelling like street
grime and spaghetti sauce.

If going to Pollsmoor prison maximum security was a shock,
this night proved to be different, yet just as powerful. We met
together for singing and prayer as usual.

I love coloured women. Singing out in all sorts of keys,
dancing and clapping, they sang with the urgency and pain of
mothers and grandmothers whose loved ones lived behind
these bars.

A coloured lady next to me with perfect white teeth, structured cheekbones, and olive skin stood to say something. I expected a "hello, nice to see everyone," introduction. Instead, she began with, "When I was in Pollsmoor in 2008, I heard the singing from a prayer walk and that's when God really grabbed my heart." Now, here she was, a free woman, coming back to do her own prayer walk.

The pastor who was leading the opening meeting, sporting a white Izod sweater vest and a plaid button-down, concluded with, "I was sentenced to 30 years, but by God's grace I only served seven." So that was what redemption looked like – a return to the place of wounding to offer a lifeline.

I later watched him dance, jump and sing at the top of his lungs through the dark prison courtyards, waving his arms, proclaiming the same possibilities to this younger generation. It is one of the powerful moves of God, to return to the captives with the brilliant news of the recently freed.

They didn't tell us that this time the prisoners would be close enough to reach out and touch us. Of Pollsmoor's nearly eight thousand inmates, 800 were young men between the ages of 14-21. If the men were loud, the boys were downright ROWDY.

Unlike the last visit, we weren't confined to the outdoor courtyard but we were able to walk inside the corridors of the cell blocks. Every shout, yell and whistle bounced between the cement walls like a small gymnasium packed with team rivals.

Prisoners on both sides, 60 people and an accordion inside a passageway; all wanting their message to be heard. We behaved like a cramped jar of fireflies set to polka music. Yet, amazingly, when we asked the boys to be quiet so we could let them know that we had not lost hope for them, they quieted immediately.

The small square windows to each block stood about 4 feet from the ground, surrounded by brick and cement. As we began praying and walking through the cell blocks, hands squeezed from underneath the windows, in between the bars.

Hands stretched through, grasping for someone to touch. Some were covered with tattoos, others wore plastic jelly bracelets. They stretched their hands toward us as if asking the unspoken question, "Could you love me? Could you accept me? Could you show me hope?"

"Please, pray for me, my seestah." At first, I was hesitant to touch their hands, I mean on *Law and Order* touching of prisoners wasn't allowed. But, I soon saw it for the honor that it was. Even though I couldn't see clearly through the bars and the clouded window, I wanted to make sure my hands answered their questions. Yes. Yes. Yes.

I held onto those hands. Baby hands. Hands that should have been grasping an Xbox controller or a rugby ball. Instead, they had inflicted untold pain, undoubtedly a response to a pain inflicted on them. Over and over, touching, praying, grasping, soothing, holding.

Outside in the prison courtyards, where the bars are a bit wider, the smaller boys sat on the window ledge, sticking their legs out the window, between the bars, letting their stockinged feet hang down. One of our ladies walked over to the bare legs, reached up and tickled the bottom of the feet. High pitched giggles erupted as the feet automatically recoiled and kicked the night air.

Over and over, from block to block, until all 800 boys were prayed over, we kept at it. Just when I thought I was too exhausted to continue, there was another cell block waiting. It looked hopeless. Utterly, despicably, darkly, hopeless. There was so much hunger. But not enough feeding.

At one point I noticed Kevin, dressed in his black Under Armor hoodie, had a monster grasp on a young pair of hands squeezed through the cell window. With one hand, he was holding hands through the bars and the other hand was planted flat against the wall in a football defense stance like a linebacker as if he was going to pray that wall right down or charge through it to hold that boy in his arms. I caught myself thinking, "I'm so glad my kids are not in prison."

Then I realized, these are my kids. There is no such thing as someone else's children. These kids are a product of the society in which I live and breath. These kids are my kids. These are my boys. THESE ARE MY BOYS. These are *your* boys. These are *our* boys.

As we left one cell block, a row of hands extended out the windows and clapped in unison. "Thank you, thank you!" they yelled. They applauded as we walked. They applauded.

20

Who Steals THAT?!

The robb'd that smiles, steals something from
the thief;
He robs himself that spends a bootless grief.

William Shakespeare

OUR VAN WAS SITTING with our mechanic, Stanley for repair, yet again. It had to be at least 15 times now. Owning a 1987 Volkswagen Microbus was not as cool as it sounded. This was the second engine rebuild and it still sporadically misbehaved for attention like a D-list reality star.

Oh, it looked groovy alright, but it was unreliable mechanically and a pain to drive. It required some unconventional methods to coax the old gal into responding. The engine was in the boot, as you know, with VW's.

Sometimes the engine liked to start when requested. Other times, we had to knock on the engine manifold with a pair of metal barbecue tongs to spark it to life. When the van wouldn't start, someone would yell, "Get the tongs" and everyone knew it wasn't for a cookout.

I've had to push it uphill in a skirt and flip flops and we've had to call numerous friends for help. We even had the tow truck guy on speed dial. One time, while shopping at the mall, the dubious decision was made to park the old gal in the underground parking lot. You know, the fancy one that requires a ticket so the toll gate would open to let you through.

Lo and behold, what did you know, after we loaded our groceries and piled into the van, we sat in agitated silence while Kevin tried to start the van. Nothing, not even the metal tong outburst would persuade her to start. We called the towing company who recognized our number on caller ID.

We waited a good few hours for the tow truck to arrive while our groceries wilted in the heat. Our friend, Jean, arrived to keep us company and talked me down from the tantrum that was brewing as I watched other people get into their cars and drive off like that was normal.

They were so haughty the way they pointed their wireless remotes toward their vehicle which beeped in happy recognition like Pavlov's dog.

When the tow truck driver arrived in a flatbed truck, we watched in abject horror as he tried to maneuver unsuccessfully through the low clearance of the underground parking garage. As we watched him give up and park outside we realized with unfolding bewilderment that he would not be able to get to us. We were going to have to go to him.

I don't know if you've ever had to push an old Microbus out of a busy, underground parking garage, but it can really try the patience. There were no kids with us so it was up to me, Kevin and Jean to wangle this temperamental beast into daylight.

We got the joy of maneuvering around parked cars while waiting for space to clear just long enough to get enough momentum going to make it up the incline to the exit ramp before the thing rolled back down onto one of us. Alas, there was one thing we forgot in our master plan – the toll gate.

We had a good amount of momentum going and didn't want to stop the van to pay. Nor did we fancy crashing through it. In a brilliant flash of dexterity and athleticism, Jean ran ahead of the Microbus, fed the parking ticket into the meter as we estimated the opening of the gate perfectly, just in time to sail through it.

I use the word 'sail' liberally here as the maximum speed achieved while pushing a Microbus uphill through a parking garage was less than optimal.

After that, we temporarily drove a much nicer and newer van by at least a decade. Friends in South Africa went to the US for the summer and we got to use their car. Glory to Jesus because it had a radio, turn signals, and brakes - all the luxuries.

Unfortunately, Kevin came out of the house one morning only to find that the side window had been shattered. The van was parked directly in front of our house and of course, we were home at the time.

Bing said they used the broken ceramic part of a spark plug to somehow break the glass without sound. We'd been driving it for all of two weeks and this happened... I swear there was a curse on us and cars.

The most irritating thing was that we couldn't figure out what they stole. The radio was still there. The ashtray still had coins in it. The only thing missing was one child's shoe. The family we borrowed the van from had little kids so they had likely left little people shoes in the car.

The crooks didn't have the decency to take the pair, they took one blimey shoe. One. The left one to be exact. Now we not only had to pay to repair the window, but we also had to go shoe shopping.

21

The Not So Good Samaritan

Another morning and I wake with thirst for the
goodness I do not have...

Mary Oliver

LATE AFTERNOON on a mild winter Cape Town day, I
coerced Kevin into taking a walk around our neighborhood. It
was kind of an intense path that involved stairs, lots of stairs.
My mind stayed focused on trying not to collapse from lack
of oxygen.

As we descended the hill and I could breathe again, I saw her,
sitting on the curb, shuffling her feet in the gravel. The bobby
pins in her hair held certain sections more adamantly than
others. Her pants were cotton brown, the shade of a milk
chocolate bar that's been lost in the pantry for months and
suddenly found.

In mid-breath, about five steps away from her, I felt a small
voice inside me say, "Stop for this one."
Wait...What?... Now?

I WASN'T IN THE MOOD FOR THIS TODAY!

I smiled a cheery hello to her. She seemed surprised. She held out her cupped hand for money and with a sound that only comes from a mouth unhindered by teeth, said, "Can you help me, please?" I did not stop. I passed right on by.

I know what you're thinking. You're looking at this scenario as if it happened in your own neighborhood. Perhaps you are viewing this from small-town America, homeless population of two. And one of those is an angst-y hipster with a point to prove, so he doesn't count. You're aghast. It's ok, you can judge.

It was not the first time that day I had been asked for money. Five, six, seven times a day it happened. Every day. At the stoplights. At the post office. At the grocery stores. At the library. In the McDonald's drive-thru. At the mall...

But...

As I walked by, I knew immediately it was a mistake. Within the space of ten steps, I both heard the plea to help and felt the sting of guilt when I chose to ignore it. *Oh, come on!*

Why does God do that? If perhaps I had been prepared before the walk, I would have been ready. I wouldn't have expended so much energy trying to convince my noodled thighs to take one more step.

God, would it be too much to ask for a pre-game pep talk? This was an ambush. I didn't start my walk with the intention to stop and help anyone. I set out with the intention to conquer some stairs and burn some calories. That morning was supposed to be all about me.

That person who walked by without helping...that wasn't the

me I wanted people to meet. At that moment I was the not-so-good-Samaritan. In a flash, I went from thinking about my grocery list to carrying a crap bag full of guilt, regret, and self-condemnation along with the dawning horror that I had come to the point where I could consciously choose *not* to help.

No matter if I encountered two or 20 people a day, I was susceptible to the slow calcification process of a soft heart subtly turning into a heart of stone. It took this one out-of-place lady, sitting on the curb for me to realize how soft Truth's whisper was and how loudly my own selfishness responded.

I understood the parable of the Good Samaritan found in the gospel of Luke. I have been all four characters at one time or another. I've been the person lying on the side of the road, beaten and robbed, raising a feeble hand to see if anyone would stop to help.

I've been the Priest and Levite who walked by, filled with pride and its sinister counterparts, self-loathing and condemnation. I've been the Good Samaritan, the one who stopped.

The Good Samaritan was not just a one-time event. We all have played or will play the roles of each character. Some roles we hang on to a bit more dogmatically than others. Do you know what I learned most from the parable of the Good Samaritan?

The person lying on the ground was not always the one in need of rescue. Often the one in need of rescue was the one walking by.

22

Shane

Here is what we seek: a compassion that can
stand in awe at what the poor have to carry
rather than stand in judgment at how they
carry it.

Gregory Boyle

I BAKE cinnamon rolls once a year. If you were thinking I said, "I bake once a year," that would also not be too far from the truth. First of all, Christmas in the southern hemisphere is in the heat of summer. It's more of a beach day with ice cream cones than baked goods and pine trees. Nevertheless, I baked because it reminded us of snow days, fireplaces and a Bing Crosby (not my neighbor) Christmas.

The week before Christmas, somewhere between baking cinnamon rolls and trying to remember if I had equal gifts for every child in our family, there was a knock at the door.

With the sticky dough on my hands and flour racing down the front of my shirt, I opened the door, silently condemning the unfortunate soul who showed up here unannounced. I had a strict pop-in policy: don't do it. I'm an introvert, people. Surprise visits give me a rash. Despite the psychosomatic hives, there was one person who always popped in, and I usually made an exception for him.

At least once a month he hobbled up to our front steps with his cane and his case of trash bags for sale, and at least once a month I bought his overpriced black, plastic rolls that smelled like a rubber factory. I could have bought them cheaper in the store.

These at least were black, rolled nicely and taped with a thank you note. "God Bless You, Shane" was written in shaky handwriting along with a phone number to call in a trash bag emergency. Interesting, since I knew he didn't own a phone.

For about a year we'd maintained this relationship where he offered trash bags that may or may not have been stolen and I bought them whether I needed them or not. He rode the train from the other side of Cape Town to hand-deliver these trash bag bundles. Mind you, he didn't pay to ride the train. He hopped on in between stops and dodged authority, which wasn't hard to do.

Sometimes he was incorrigible. Other times he reeked of cheap wine. He was always smoking. His fingers were yellow, covered with callouses and overgrown nails. He wore silver rings on most of his fingers.

I couldn't imagine that he maintained a huge trash bag clientele in the valley. But for some reason, he made the trek. There was something about him; something that stuck in my heart. His hair was naturally blonde, buzzed neatly with sideburns. At 42, he still had freckles sprinkled over high cheek-bones, emphasized by his gaunt face.

If he put on a few pounds, his skin would fill out what's left of a sculptured jawline. He was good looking once. Now his teeth had a piano key pattern - alternating between black and white. He always wore white clothes which emphasized his tan and his watery blue eyes. He wore two thin gold hoops in each ear which peeked out from underneath a white Nike mesh hat.

I quickly tried to dust the flour off my shirt, which resulted in a successful smearing of it everywhere. I opened the door expecting to make a quick purchase of my usual hand-delivered trash bags.

Right away, I knew something was not right. I noticed he had none of his trademark attire. For starters, he was wearing women's flip flops. They used to be red once but were now sun faded to pink. The ornamental flower was missing and in its place sat a stub that rose from a rough plastic hollow stem.

Secondly, when I asked about the trash bags, he hung his head and held out four solitary bags.

A couple of months ago God asked me to stop and help a lady but I didn't have time for that. Today I thought, no. I would not miss an opportunity for something extraordinary again. I motioned for him to sit on the front porch.

"Do you want anything to drink?" I asked.

"Wine."

"I don't have wine."

"Oh, sorry, I didn't know there was another option."

"I'm bringing you juice and a sandwich."

He shuffled to the porch, looked across the road where he'd just come from and sat with his head down. At first, the usual stuff came out...kicked out of this place... robbed...took his clothes...out of jail on bail...but they weren't his drugs... well...not all of them, some were his.

I listened.

Lurking behind my hesitation to do good was the fear of being deceived. Being deceived was a fear that kept me away from the front lines; away from all the real action before.

Other than overpriced trash bags, the only thing Shane had ever asked for was some ibuprofen the day he showed up with a gaping head wound after being attacked with a golf club. I would have rather taken the risk of being conned than missing out on a beautiful moment.

I asked God to give me something to say to Shane. I had learned that the key to a deeper relationship with God was walking through the door of risk and inconvenience. So I took the risk.

Shane could very well think that I'm the one who was nuts, talking to God and all. Maybe we both were out of our damn minds. After all, I was the one coated in baking flour like a chicken drumstick sitting on my front porch thinking that God wanted to say something to Shane through me.

I spoke a few words to him—ones I thought God was bringing to my mind because it definitely wasn't anything that I came up with on my own. It did not include anything about life choices and consequences, just the opposite.

The next thing I knew, he was crying. It was a powerful thing —believing God used me to speak to someone. We could tell someone that God loves them all we want. But when Love speaks through words and pictures that only that person will understand, it goes straight to the heart.

It wasn't often that a proud man broke down in tears on my front porch and admitted to being a homeless 'chemist' for a local drug lord, who lived in both fear and loathing of his own life.

At that moment, what God wanted to talk about was not Shane's present or past. God chose to remind Shane about his future. Sometimes we get so overwhelmed sifting through the gutters of tragedy that we don't look up to see the streams of living water rushing toward us in cleansing waves.

That's what I got to do. I got the gift of speaking hope and joy into an empty well of a man - a well that had long since dried up and been abandoned. I got to live from the future and bring it into the present.

It reminded me of the story of Jesus and the Samaritan woman at the well. I love that story. Jesus didn't make her explain every past humiliation and shame, standing before the congregation in repentance, wearing a scarlet letter A, and signing a contract agreeing to a year's worth of accountability and counseling from a stalwart of the faith.

Instead, sitting by that well, He let her in on the greatest news the world was yet to hear. And she was the one who got to break the news to an unbelieving world.

Shane let me pray with him for a good long time. He closed his eyes, arms extended, palms turned upwards, barely breathing with tears sitting in the creases of his face. I could see the water of life begin to flow again in that sacred moment.

Joy is a transforming mystery - a floodgate of restoration; an unleashed dam of cascading kindness that reached deep, deep within his spirit. He didn't leave the same person. Instead of being agitated and fidgety, he stood peacefully, his eyes calm. He hugged me tightly. There was a smile and a look of disbelief as if he had no idea what just happened.

I knew what happened. He encountered peace, hope, and redemption. He encountered Jesus at the well.

23

Easy Come, Easy Go

You're turning me into a criminal when all I
want to be is a petty thug.

Bart Simpson

IT WAS NOT out of the ordinary for our car mechanic to pay us a house visit. He dropped by often for a cup of tea or an exhaust manifold. We had a co-dependent relationship, you might say. He came to our rescue like an obstetrician on call. It was like we put out a bat signal in the sky and Stanley just knew where to find us.

Stanley was the last of our mechanics because he'd been what the other mechanics had not been - trustworthy. He'd even driven 45 minutes just to rescue us from the side of the road, stranded.

One day, we gloriously received a miracle. After years of driving one untrustworthy VW Microbus, we found an answer to prayer. A SsangYong Musso, a Korean model, 7-

seater SUV, automatic (a luxury!) appeared on the local face-book page for sale.

The price range was well below the typical cost of cars in South Africa for that size and condition. I mean, we had squeezed into Jasmine, the Ford Fiesta Car of the Year. To be able to stretch out these 6-feet tall frames in an SUV would be amazing. It was a whole decade younger than the VW that had failed us more times than an Independent running for president.

We quickly extended the offer to our supports and asked if they would be willing to help us buy the vehicle. Knowing our ongoing battle with transportation, people quickly and generously gave several thousands of dollars for us to be able to buy this car.

One person gave us a portion of their inheritance money! It happened so quickly, it had to be a divinely approved operation.

We test drove the car with the seller, a guy our age. We met his wife. He offered us tea. We quite liked him and there was something quite charming and familiar about him. Oh yes, we'd seen him a few times at a local church we visited from time to time. He loved this car, he said, but financially, he and his wife needed to sell it to pay for his hospital bills.

He showed us pictures of his former self at prime health. He'd obviously been sick for some time now. He asked if we would be willing to pray for him. Sure, we said. He'd love for us to be the buyers, as there was indeed, a lot of interest on the facebook group and he really liked us. He felt like God wanted us to have it.

He reduced the price further and offered us the car right then.

From the moment we saw the Facebook ad, to raising the funds, to meeting the guy, to signing papers, everything opened up to us and proceeded so smoothly, it could only be the right thing for us to do.

We quickly bought the car and loved everything about it.

For 48 hours.

The black smoke from the exhaust pipe started stinking up the roadway, followed by a loud commotion from the engine. We called Stanley and he quickly came over and seemed troubled. He had a few ideas but would need some time to take the engine apart.

A few days later, he came back with dreadful news. Our car curse had followed us and the engine of this car would need to be totally replaced or rebuilt.

We went back to the original seller and told him the car was defective. He insisted that he didn't have the money any longer, because he had already spent the cash on his hospital bills. We sat with the news that we had been swindled into buying a colossal lemon of a car. There was no refund coming. We had just lost $7000. We felt like God had pulled a fast one on us.

There was some hope. "The body of the car was great, the tires were new, the interior was leather, it was worth saving," Stanley said.

"Ok, what are we looking at, cost-wise," Kevin asked.

"I can get a used engine and build it into this one. It won't be new but it will run. It will take me a couple of weeks to do it, once I find the right parts. It will cost about R25000 ($2000).

I will need a 50% deposit so I can start the work and buy the parts."

We got a pretty good deal on the car, and even if you factored in the cost of a new engine, it was still below market price for a car this size and this year. I mean, it was a 1989 model, which for us, was as good as new. We agreed to follow Stanley's' advice and rebuild the engine. Kevin brought him the deposit money and we waited.

And waited.

And waited.

Three weeks later Stanley paid us an unexpected visit at home. He was quite apologetic about the car. It was taking longer than he expected and it was not as straightforward as he would've liked. Once he got in there, he could see that several mechanics had already tried their hand at this car and none seemed to have succeeded.

Three weeks later…

Stanley seemed troubled as he stood in our lounge that night. He said his ex-wife had caused some drama with his kids and he was going to have to go to court. He was really short on cash. This last month, there had been several riots around the area where Stanley's shop was located, in an industrial park.

Residents had been setting tires alight, looting and damaging neighboring businesses. As a result, no one had been able to enter the industrial park and several businesses were unable to operate, including Stanley's.

Three weeks later…

He desperately needed the remaining 50% of the deposit if he was to continue. With the riots, he had not been paid in a while. He hated to ask but could we please pay the full amount to help him get through this dry spell, which was unforeseeable. Stanley was near tears as he leaned against the wall and covered his face with his hands.

Of course, if we could help out and get him back on his feet, we would do that. Kevin went into our safe, otherwise known as the space between our bed mattresses, and retrieved the remaining money. We had planned to use it to pay rent, but this seemed a bit more pressing.

Two weeks. He was busy, swamped with clients.

Another two weeks. There had been a few South African holidays so no one was actually working.

Two weeks and two days. Kevin called for an update but there was no answer. Or text. Stanley was never at his shop when we visited.

Two weeks and five days. It was Saturday but Kevin drove past Stanley's garage again. There was a craft brewery next door and as Kevin was peering into the window of Stanley's garage, one of the guys said, "He's not here, haven't seen him in a while." Maybe there was a family emergency and he was visiting Durban.

Over four months after we bought the car…

On Monday, we both went to Stanley's garage. We were greeted by a group of women who sold spicy samosas and cool drinks to the industrial park employees.

"He's not here, he's long gone. Everyone is looking for him."

"What do you mean, gone?" Kevin asked. "Like gone for good? Gone for the weekend?"

"Gone for good. He won't be back. There's a new guy moving into his rental space today."

What? Someone else was going to rent the garage? Where was our SUV?

After a few minutes, a guy in his mid-fifties arrived. He was wearing dark blue denim jeans with a denim button-down shirt tucked in neatly. His brown leather belt served as the equator amidst a sea of blue. His shoes were white tennis shoes with mesh sides and a rubber wedge heel. His hands were like two slices of sandpaper when we shook hands.

He introduced himself to us as the new tenant of the garage. He was here today to prepare the area for his paint company to take ownership of the garage space.

"I'm so glad I don't have to track down the owner of this car. There were a few others, but this is a big one," he said, referring to our SUV. As he opened the garage door, we saw our dream SUV in the sickbay.

There was our sad car, in a thousand pieces all over the garage floor like a neurotic jigsaw puzzle. Gone was our mechanic, gone was our money, gone was our car.

Stunned doesn't begin to describe our reaction. Angry, hysterical, devastated and betrayed were hovering on the surface with a few expletives breaking ground. The paint guy in double denim had little sympathy.

"If it makes you feel any better, there are a few bad types also looking for this guy. Looks like he skipped town with a lot of unfinished business and a lot of money. If he comes back here, he won't survive long, if you know what I mean."

I did know what he meant and it most certainly did *not* make me feel any better.

"Oh my word, what are we supposed to do?" I asked as if either one of us had been in that situation before.

Double denim chimed in, "My business moves into this space today, so if you could move the car out of here, that would be great."

I had never had the burning desire to throat punch someone more than this very moment. I glared at him, glared at the floor and back at him until he made the obvious connection.

"If I were you, I'd call the insurance company and claim it was stolen." He checked over his shoulder and whispered, "Just leave it near here, someone will help themselves to it in no time if you know what I mean."

I did know what he meant and I didn't think that was what I felt comfortable telling the insurance company. Thank goodness we had it insured though. We called a tow truck to have the shell towed to yet another mechanic who agreed to let us store it at his place until we could figure out what the sam hill to do.

Meanwhile, friends arrived with several plastic bins and shoveled pieces and car parts into indistinct piles of metal. To watch what you thought was your answer to prayer be loaded into Rubbermaid bins was not a good way to end the week.

I called the insurance company and told them the whole story. They told us to file a police report. We walked into the police station. The detective wrote down our details in a little flip-top notebook and said he would look into the missing mechanic scenario.

It didn't escape my notice that he didn't take down the address of Stanley's garage. He also said that he would not be investigating a theft of any sort.

"You gave the guy the keys to the vehicle when you brought the car to him, correct?"

"Yes, we did."

"It's not theft then, is it, if you gave him the keys?"

We didn't acquire the necessary police report to give the insurance company, although I did acquire a swollen tongue as a result of biting it. The insurance company had no intention of paying for a car that went missing but wasn't technically stolen.

Basically, we lost the car...twice. That week was not my favorite week in South Africa.

Like a bad infomercial...but wait, there's more...

24

It Just So Happened

O me, you juggler, you canker-blossom, you
thief of love!

William Shakespeare

IT WAS NEARLY midnight and the house was quiet. Everyone was asleep. I was using this peaceful time at the edges of the day to sift through my thoughts on life.

Tonight, I "just so happened" to walk through the lounge (living room area) on my way to the kitchen. I just so happened to have the urge to look outside to make sure the boogie man wasn't lurking in our bushes.

Lo, and behold, he was lurking! The actual boogie man made an appearance wearing tan capri pants and a powder blue sweatshirt. Under the porch light, I could see a male figure walking in front of the VW van which was parked in front of the garage. My first thought was, "Oh, someone must be coming to visit," which would be normal if it wasn't midnight.

I saw this guy walking around the van and slowly realized that indeed, I DID NOT KNOW THIS MAN. He motioned to someone in the distance as if to say, 'come here.' Sure enough, I saw three silhouettes spring from a small car on the opposite side of the street, jogging our way.

Hold up, what was happening? Why were these guys coming to our house, surrounding our van?

Clarity dawned and adrenaline kicked in. We had a car stolen out from underneath our noses while we were home before so I am familiar with this storyline. Without much thought, I yelled for Kevin to come downstairs, forthwith.

He was in a deep sleep so I wasn't sure if he even heard me, understood me or thought I was dream nagging. I flung open the front door and marched myself outside *in my Ohio State pajamas* to inquire, in an as polite manner as possible, what this man and his friends thought they were doing.

The guy in capri pants looked at me and ducked around the corner where I couldn't see him. They all must have run in the opposite direction because I couldn't see any of them. I ran inside to get my cell phone.

My first call was to my neighbor, Bing Crosby and Neighborhood Watch, the special forces of public safety. Bing had retired for the night but realized she forgot her cell phone in the lounge so she woke up and walked to the lounge to get it at the very moment I just so happened to be calling.

Bing called in the reinforcements of Neighborhood Watch on her 24-hour surveillance walkie/talkie. A very tough looking guy named Andre just so happened to be monitoring our road at the very moment he received the call on the walkie talkie.

He spotted suspicious activity on our road, noted the license plate of a suspicious car and followed the car which just so happened to be the getaway car that the boogie man and his boogie buddies were driving.

Neighborhood Watch camera crew were able to see that the suspicious car had been reported stolen earlier that evening.

So of course, Andre and the Neighborhood Watch on duty pulled over the getaway car on Main Road. No really, Neighborhood Watch made the car stop and pull over for questioning. Within ten minutes, they had four guys handcuffed face down on the pavement in front of Scooter's Pizza.

Bing quietly knocked on my front door to let me know that Neighborhood Watch wanted a witness statement from me so could I please come to Scooter's Pizza to identify these guys?

Um no. I was done for the night. I was already comfy in my pajamas. I didn't have a car to get there because the thieves ripped open the steering column and jammed a screwdriver into the ignition switch and it was too mangled to use.

"No problem," Bing said, "I can take you on my scooter or Andre will come back and get you and take you to the site." "Oh goody," I thought. "Could this even be real?" By now, Kevin was awake, sitting downstairs.

He was quite miffed at the damage done to the van in the attempted break-in. It was not like we weren't still licking our wounds from earlier this week. I jumped into Andre's car, which was a Volkswagen Chico with sirens on the roof. He wore a bulletproof vest with a retractable baton.

There was a Guy Fawkes mask in the seat next to me and I

was mesmerized thinking, "Who is this mystery man of the Neighborhood Watch?" It was a juicy reality show waiting to happen.

An hour before, I had thought my day was finished and I would be heading to bed. Now I was sitting in the back of a complete stranger's car driving to a pizza joint to see if I could identify the right capri pants in a lineup.

I was laughing so hard to myself that I had to look out the window to keep from making eye contact with Andre in the rearview mirror. Andre was all business. Andre was not laughing.

He stopped on the main road where a crowd has gathered. I walked up to see four guys sprawled on the pavement with zip ties holding their hands behind their backs. I wondered if they knew they were apprehended by a Neighborhood Watch volunteer group.

The police were on the scene now, their lorry parked in the middle of the road. I tried to decide if these were the guys I saw in front of my house AS THEY WERE WATCHING ME IDENTIFY THEM!

So much for a one-way safety mirror. People were walking past carrying steaming bacon and cheese pizzas as I was staring at criminals and wondering if they would remember where I live once they made bail.

The investigator on duty arrived with a notebook with carbon paper in between each page. I relayed the same story to him as best as I could recall. He wrote the same details on three sets of paper.

I asked him if he could command the guy to come back and

fix the van. I mean, he was just going to be sitting in jail right now anyway. It was a chance for restitution and we might as well put his obvious mechanical skills to good use.

He said no. So now we couldn't drive our van until it was fixed.

25

Fire On the Mountain, Run Boys Run

The pines were roaring on the heights, The
   wind was moaning in the night,
The fire was red, it flaming spread, The trees
   like torches blazed with light.

J.R.R. Tolkein

I AWAKENED to the taste of ash on my lips. Our windows
didn't fully seal and the glass was paper thin. The smell of
smoke gave me an automatic headache. The mountains
behind us were on fire. I don't mean like Pentecostal tongues.
Literally, they were burning.

That was the summer of fires for our area. Thousands of hectares
of wild, indigenous brush were reduced to black, glossy grave-
yards. A combination of the parched earth and vicious summer
winds outmatched the fire department at every turn. The wind
kept the helicopters grounded and the firetrucks from the mountain passes. The ongoing drought left water levels depleted.

We lived at the low end of the mountain range which was currently ablaze. We watched it burn with a wary eye as it made its way closer to us. Several rows of houses separated us from the inferno.

One thing I loved was the fact that Bing hopped on her scooter and went to the aid of the fire department. When their radio system failed, she became the carrier pigeon between the fire station and firefighters, riding her scooter between the two, relaying messages.

Local people set up areas of respite for the firefighters in community centers and churches. They brought bottles of water, sandwiches and first aid to the firefighters as they came in for water breaks. It was such a lovely gesture of gratitude to watch unfold.

This was at least our fourth blaze of the year. The first time we saw helicopters dropping buckets of water from the sky was a novelty. The second time, still fascinating. Now, it was an inconvenience of note as the gray ash left a layer of dust on window sills, kitchen dishes, and bookshelves.

By early afternoon we could see the orange and red flames making their way down the mountain directly toward us. By early evening, we were walking around the house with our mouths covered with our shirts.

While I was sitting at my desk trying to organize my life, I heard a faint voice from a megaphone outside my window. The red paint of a firetruck caught my eye. It was driving slowly down the street, pausing at each house. As it passed our house, the muffled voice became more clear.

"City of Cape Town Fire Department...Evacuate. Evacuate

your homes." The firetruck continued down the street and turned. There were no further instructions.

The VW Microbus was not running thanks to the recent attempted theft from the day before. We were under strict instructions from the police investigator to not so much as touch the vehicle until the fingerprints had been taken. It was still a crime scene.

And of course, what would have been our dream car was sitting in glorified Tupperware containers thanks to the handiwork of our disappearing mechanical act, Stanley.

This begged the question, how did one evacuate without a vehicle? With our valued belongings tucked into grocery store bags, we headed down the street on foot. If we could have tied our belongings into a kerchief and dangled them from the end of a stick, it would have been more fitting.

As we walked in a cluster, down the street, carrying important documents and such, I looked around and remembered to laugh. I seriously couldn't make this stuff up. Here we were, shuffling down the street like Emmet Otters' Jug Band Christmas, evacuating our house... on foot.

When in my life would I ever have dreamed up two car thefts, a fire and house evacuation in the same week? I was exhausted but smirking because if I didn't laugh, I'd probably commit a felony. Weeks like this made me question our decision to move to South Africa.

I have a college degree. I could have been sitting behind a desk with a cushy swivel chair. My biggest problem could have been my office partner named Patricia who did nothing but complain about Republicans and the air conditioning temperature.

We walked to the nearby house of our friends, Shawn and Dave. They gave us dinner and strong drink. I had friends who let us crash at their house smelling like a forest fire, eat their food, and then distracted us with entertainment. This was the best way that week could have ended.

26

Permission to Rage

Do not go gentle into that good night.
Rage, rage against the dying of the light.

Dylan Thomas

I MADE a Christmas salad one year. There was no signifi-
cance in calling it a Christmas salad except that I made it on
Christmas and it had all the trademarks of a salad. It was for
our annual Christmas lunch with our American friends, Dave
and Shawn. I detest cooking so my food was not only a minor
Christmas miracle, it was Facebook worthy.

That picture received 60 likes. My pile of lettuce and pine
nuts received 60 digital thumbs up. My salad in a cracked
bowl attracted enough attention to not only get likes but
comments as well. In fact, over 30 people took the time to
maintain an ongoing dialogue about my salad. In all fairness,
it did have cranberries, so it was quite fetching.

Here's the thing, I don't know if it was the holiday blues,
homesickness, or a fissure in the volcanic crack in my petri-

fied heart that was letting out some raging steam but, when I posted that seven people had been murdered in our community that month alone, there was silence....

Crickets. Not a comment.

Where was the collective outrage? It takes the same amount of effort to think about salad as it does homicide. Was it compassion fatigue? Too many stories so we numbed ourselves, insulated away from pain? Was it that you'd never met my friends, didn't know the community and didn't know what to say?

Did that same set of emotions allow you to feel something toward my salad but not toward my heartache? Were you afraid of pain? Feeling it? Holding it? Sharing it? Was it because they were not your friends, family, ethnicity, or fellow countrymen?

Have we forgotten that geography is a man-made boundary but humanity is eternal? Since when have we resorted to lowering our heads, shrugging our shoulders and escaping into digital non-reality where it's beautiful and nothing hurts? Vonnegut would be so proud.

When was the last time you stopped scrolling through social media, read a story that made you weep in agony, and cried out to God on behalf of someone else's heartache? How often do you let yourself go into a blind rage, in pain for an unknown person?

I'm not talking about a personal offense but a universal injustice that won't benefit you in the slightest to fight. It feels like we are being coaxed, reasoned and numbed into looking away from injustice only to become fixated on manufactured lifestyles of the bon vivant instead.

Defiance in the face of injustice is inspiring, beautiful, coura-geous and contagious. But we must see the injustice in real life, not on the Internet or TV as if it's a well-produced reality show.

I'm learning that I don't have to solve injustice. I just have to see it, and look into the eyes of the evil system that props it up with with rational words and economic security, and then talks me down from my outrage with the lull from a faint hymn and a Bible verse.

Where are those of us who will walk into the temples, flip the tables and drive the empire from the sacred?

Brokenness isn't presented to us without reason. Inside that brokenness are the very pieces of ourselves that we are miss-ing. When we stop, see, and step in to help another, it benefits us too. It's here that we tangibly see, feel, and experience God. He is already here, in the very brokenness I sometimes deem unworthy of my effort.

Do you want to feel the love of God? Sit next to a person who slept on the street, help him clean sewer water from his belongings and then take him out for breakfast. That experi-ence right there – that's a lesson from God.

You will not be able to offer a solution to his complicated life. But that experience is for you to see the face of Jesus. These moments are only rich if we take the time to step in, be present and allow it to take our breath away.

If I do it right, I will gasp and choke and cry and rage and exhale and inhale and breathe and live. Most of all, I will rage again.

Somehow, as we get older we become tamed, controlled and

contained. But what if the opposite should be true? What if the more we see God, the more we remember our call to be outrageously wild?

Why have we allowed ourselves to be tamed?

When did we shut the gate of possibility?

When did we resign ourselves to the ordinary or rational?

When did the justification "but" wedge itself into our psyche?

If we say we follow the teaching and example of a Palestinian refugee who defied the system, why have we lulled ourselves back to sleep?

When did we start believing that the smaller, cleaner, safer story was good enough?

When did my stupid cranberry salad become so interesting?

27

Tackling a Drug Lord

Question authority.

Socrates

ONE SUMMER IN NOVEMBER, Hudson and his soccer mates participated in a huge soccer tournament. It was the largest one of the year, held on the other side of Cape Town. There were 32 teams. Some arrived in fancy decked-out team buses.

Others, like us, arrived in crowded city taxis. This tournament was so prestigious in the Western Cape province that there was a drill team and marching band performing on the field. When Hudson played for the Crew Juniors, a soccer club in Columbus, we never had a team bus or even a marching band.

During the semi-finals, things got pretty heated on the sidelines between one particularly rowdy, opinionated parent and the center referee. If you've ever been to a kid's soccer game, you know this is nothing new. There's always that one parent or ten.

Kevin stood on the sidelines, close to the action. All of a sudden, a hefty looking guy from the opposing team wearing jeans and a blue t-shirt ran onto the field, screaming obscenities in Afrikaans. Generously, there were international gestures for those of us who required a translation.

Having articulately voiced his disagreement, the hefty guy resorted to another form of communication and suddenly took an off-balanced swing at the referee. Our coach ran over to stop the assault but was instead hit by Hefty. The athletes lifted their heads from the soccer pitch, the ball slowly rolled to a stop as they slowly congregated around this bizarre mayhem.

Kevin quietly and quickly hustled into the chaos and restrained the irate guy in a giant bear hug. Feeling that he was outsized, Hefty calmed down long enough to be escorted off the field by police. As he was leaving the field, he suddenly turned and, with a giant fist, punched a little girl playing with her stuffed animals on the sidelines.

The game ended right then.

The police grabbed the guy and put him in handcuffs, stuffing him into the back of a police car. The referees left with haste. Our team advanced to the finals by default. We were winning anyway, for the record.

A few days later, Kevin got a call from our club's coach. Turns out, this fancy opposing team, with the fancy buses and marching band, was somehow supposedly linked to a major drug cartel in the area, or so the rumor said. The guy Kevin tackled was purportedly one of the star players in this heinous game. When Kevin relayed this information to me, all our kids listened intently.

At the realization that Kevin tackled a drug dealer, all chaos broke out, like a WWF champion had just walked into the ring. There may have been some encouragement to take a victory lap while someone ran to find a fog machine and strobe lights.

Kevin's reply was, "When I had him in that hold, he didn't feel like he had that much authority." It was only after the fact, that he stopped to consider what the consequences could have been.

There was a life lesson in there somewhere. Sometimes, we delegate authority to people who have no business being regarded as highly as we think they should be. Sometimes we give away our own authority because we don't believe we carry as much authority as we do.

Had Kevin known the history or reputation of this man, he may have thought twice before doing the right thing. But instinct kicked in and he automatically acted. Because the soccer sidelines were filled with volatile emotions and tempers, had he reacted as something other than a peacemaker the scene would have ended quite differently.

I am challenged that in matters of justice, often I seek to understand the earthly authority and bow to the rational decision rather than trusting my own spiritual authority. It's our Western mindset, of course, to analyze, criticize, and rationalize decisions, whether it's what we order at the drive-thru window or our next job opportunity. It's good and has a purpose. However, sometimes this caution will kill us from the inside.

Unless you're wailing on a piñata, swinging at a moving

target while blindfolded is a sign of immense vulnerability. I sometimes wonder what my life would look like if every time I heard the whisper of God, I listened to that deep passion inside instead of arguing my way out of it.

What if I closed my eyes and jumped more often?

28

Peep-less Easter

The audacity of hope becomes either the class
privilege that protects the chosen from the
realities of Friday or the opium used by the
poor to numb the pain of oppression until
Sunday's good news.

Miguel A. DeLaTorre

THERE ARE no Peeps in South Africa. Those who know me, know that I have a manic obsession with the iconic sugary goodness that makes its appearance every Easter. Ever since I was a little girl, the brightly colored goodness meant two things: Easter and spring. Nothing says Jesus is alive like a bunny-shaped, coma-inducing, saccharine-laced marshmallow.

It was the week before our first Easter and there were zero Peeps on the shelves. In fact, if the main grocery store was Walmart, the Easter section could have fit into a grocery cart or two.

There was also no spring. In fact, when Easter arrives on the calendar, it means winter was on its way. For the record, there was no Easter bunny in the mall taking pictures with little kids. I could not find an Easter basket to buy if I wanted one, which I did. Easter grass? Plastic eggs? Spiced jelly beans? No. No. No.

There was a small assortment of candy, mostly chocolate bunnies and white candy-covered chocolate eggs. There were no department store sales flyers advertising little girls with glossy hair, yellow dresses, and floral skirts sitting in front of smiling boys in matching polos. New Easter clothes? Not so much.

I guess all we had here was...Easter. There was a lack of hyper-consumerism related to each holiday. There was just...genuine meaning. More than half the city didn't have an Easter dinner. No ham, no egg hunts, no sugar highs.

The most noticeable thing I did have on our first Easter was energy, patience, and sleep. I was not a crabby mom who was putting on a brave face Easter morning just to get through the traditional Easter egg hunt and big lunch only to collapse in exhaustion because I stayed up most of the night organizing Easter baskets, dyeing Van Gogh-themed eggs and color coordinating floral centerpieces.

This was one of the many ways that South Africa has redeemed us from ourselves. This is the resurrection story. We couldn't rush to celebrate on Sunday when we hadn't felt the pain of Friday. For the majority of the oppressed, Sunday resurrection isa distant concept while Friday still continues.

This was a message that I needed to hear, to surrender my hopefulness coated in privilege instead of numbing my pain with yet another excessively sweet, consumer-driven distraction.

And I certainly didn't need a basket of candy.

29

A Thematic Life

Tell me, what is it you plan to do with your
one wild and precious life?

Mary Oliver

HAVE you ever caught yourself feeling a spark of curiosity or excitement about a specific person, people group or place? Maybe even a cause? You know, you try to put it out of your mind, but at random times it returns to grab your attention? You don't even know the person, or have never been to that place, but you feel a connection with it; a responsibility or longing to know more.

The first time I felt this particular connection to someone was Michael Jackson in the fifth grade. This is not what I'm talking about. That was my fifth-grade self, dreaming of being Mrs. Jackson at Neverland Ranch.

When the Syrian civil war began a few years ago, before we moved to South Africa, I read about it in passing headlines. I had a few more pressing personal obligations so it barely registered on my radar.

Fast forward to several years after we moved to South Africa, the fighting continued and stories of families fleeing Syria dominated the news.

I couldn't sit and read these incomprehensible stories and not do something. It bothered me to the point that I obsessed about how to get to these families. I spoke about it to friends, neighbors, and anyone who used oxygen. These women needed to know they were not alone.

People agreed with me. A few volunteered to go with me, but the timing was never 'just right.' What could I do besides pity and sigh and shake my head? It bothered me to the point that I researched airline prices to northern Jordan, where one of the biggest refugee camps was located.

To do what? I didn't know but at least I wouldn't be sitting around stewing in passive discontent. Something deep inside me knew that as a mother, wife, sister, I *had* to go to those women.

I somehow needed them to know that they were on my mind and in my prayers and even if the only thing I could say was, "This sucks. I hate that this is happening," then I must do that because they must know that though they might feel invisible, they are seen.

Should I go? What would I do? How would I get there? Who would pay for it? How quickly could I learn Arabic? Oh, and God, please don't ask me to go by myself. I can't find my car in a parking lot, let alone find my way through the Middle East.

I prayed and prayed. I asked for signs from God to show me that I was not losing my mind.

Here were the things I needed from God:

1. Don't ask me to go by myself. I don't speak Arabic and I have no sense of direction.

2. Can you buy a plane ticket? You're going to need to pay for this.

3. I'd like a metaphysical sign because I'm needy.

Without asking, one of our dearest and long-time financial partners gave us $1,000 without explanation to use as we needed. The airline fare came to a bit more than $800.

Another day, as we were driving down a busy highway, talking about whether or not I should go on this trip, Kevin and I started asking for a sign. At a stoplight, in the median of a busy highway, three Muslim women in burqas walked toward me in the middle of the road like that was an everyday thing. I'd take that as a sign.

Now that problems two and three had been solved, I just needed to find someone to go with me. I did what every sane person did and I posted a plea on Facebook. "Anyone who wants to go to Jordan and the refugee camps, please message me." That was a no-fail plan.

Sure enough, a friend of a friend also wanted to go, plus, she had contacts in the Middle East who could host us. What were the chances? There were five of us who planned to go initially, so we diligently met together to plot our enterprise.

But the timing came into question, yet again when there was an escalated uprising between Israel and Gaza that shook everyone and revised travel plans. Airports were closed, and travel warnings issued. Instead of a team going together, it dwindled to just my new friend Shelly, who remained committed to the trip, and me.

I mean, I already paid for the airfare. It was non-refundable. Of course, I was still going. Terrorist threats were no match for my frugality. We had no way of knowing that just weeks before our departure, Israel and Gaza would ignite in an ugly conflict (uglier than usual), ISIS would be rolling through Iraq and the Syrian fighting would become more brutal than ever.

I was kind of comfortable with the crazy. I mean, we up and moved to South Africa without jobs or a rich uncle, no offense to my uncles. Once you jump off the deep end, it gets easier each time which was why it wasn't unheard of for me to make my way to the Middle East without an agenda or goal in mind, a lot of money or even knowing a hint of Arabic. We had no humanitarian solutions or propaganda, just the desire to show love.

I inexplicably have this urge to get as close as I could to conflict and chaos. It's part of my charm. Give me a travel warning and the promise of tear gas and it's an open invitation.

My heart was drawn to my sisters who were enduring the unthinkable. Sure, I could pray and send warm feelings of love and light from home. Indeed, it would be safer, and cheaper for that matter. But I needed to go to them, to feel, to hold hands, to hold a space for them, for us.

Just two of us forty-something American women who barely knew each other, wearing long-sleeved shirts and pants in the middle of summer, boarded a plane together. After ten hours of flying, we stepped into the desert sun and made our way to a designated neighborhood in the middle of a busy, metropolitan city where we met our first contact.

It was sunset. It was the beginning of Ramadan.

And so it was, this one sweltering day I found myself sipping Arabic tea flavored with mint leaves, sitting cross-legged on a cement floor in a house close to the Syrian border...

30

Why Have You Come Here?

Everything depends on the lenses through
which we view the world. By putting on
new lenses, we can see things that would
otherwise remain invisible.

Parker J. Palmer

DON'T THINK for one minute that I didn't have second
thoughts. I mean, there I was, standing in the heart of the
Middle East in the middle of the day, walking through narrow
streets, busting at the seams.

Cars with hooting horns, rusty bicycles, grannies in dresses
so long their feet disappeared under a waterfall of material,
women carrying shopping bags filled with fresh fruit, young
kids running with mouths sticky and red, lollipops in hand,
and scruffy dogs on a mission, all traveling in various directions, and the same direction, at once.

As we approached the walkway to a modest, cement house
with old tires and pieces of trash swirling in the front yard,

we were greeted by a woman with perfectly arched eyebrows and dark eyes, wearing a hijab and multiple layers of clothing. She embraced us both, kissed us several times and flung open the doors.

Inside, there were four other women and a collection of young kids openly staring as only kids are socially permitted to do.

We sat on the cool, concrete floor together, just us women, my friend Shelly and our translator. The Arab couches provided minimal separation between my tailbone and the cement floor as we sat barefoot and cross-legged across from each other. The women sent word via skipping children that we were visiting and friends should come.

Soon, more women arrived. The hostess busied herself in the kitchen, entering and re-entering the lounge to greet each newcomer with a kiss. Chipped paint, foamy yellow, clung to the walls. A solitary picture of the Quran hung above the couches. Make-shift curtains draped the doorways as a means of separation for each family. It is a house shared between families with only a few bed mats on the floor.

The tea was refilled and fresh figs were offered. The smell of popcorn filled the chalky, desert air. We drank minty, sweet Arabic tea in small, petite glass cups with miniature handles. We ate popcorn served from tin plates held by kids serving us with chubby, dusty hands.

The hostess refused to sit down until we had been served coffee and stuffed grape leaves. Then figs. And more popcorn. Then a fruity, red drink followed by a passionate invitation to stay for dinner.

I had been informed that it was rude to refuse hospitality,

even though I knew these women had absolutely no money, no income, and little food. They opened their home, their cabinets, and their coffee pots.

More significantly, they opened their entire afternoon to us, devoting time to sit and listen to each other. Across from me sat five Syrian women, each cradling a young baby, each nursing the pain of a recent, tragic story. Quiet at first, they adjusted their hijabs and shyly fiddled with the pants underneath their abaya, the long gown that covered their clothing.

I caught a glimpse of floral print leggings underneath. Despite the temperature, they remained covered from head to toe, with the exception of bare feet. They told us who was missing from each family in a matter-of-fact tone as if to protect us from the pain of horrific loss. There were no husbands, older sons or brothers left. They were in prison, captured, killed or missing without explanation.

The faces of the children told the deeper truth.

They wore scars borne from power-hungry greed and blood-soaked deprivation. Though their little bodies resembled children, their eyes were those of survivors fleeing their holocaust.

"Why have you come here?" they asked through our translator, after sharing shocking tales of their war-torn lives. Hearing their stories was important, but that was not why we were there. My friend and I looked at each other. That was the question we'd been asking ourselves. Our translator nodded for us to begin.

"Habibti, we wanted you to know we saw what was happening to your families, to your country and what you are forced to endure. We wanted you to know that we love you and you are not forgotten. We see you and want you to know that you are not alone."

With that, they looked at each other, smiled shyly, pushed the tin of popcorn closer to us and said, "You honor us with your visit. Thank you."

From that moment, no questions were off-limits. They inquired as to why we had such short hair. They laughed at my unruly curls and frizzy hair. The kids asked to touch it.

The hijabs came off and we were treated to a lengthy demonstration of the most trendy up-dos and fashionable ways to wear one's hair underneath a headscarf. Let me just say that I had no idea that underneath a hijab could be bleached hair with aqua streaks.

The height and trajectory of the scarf was of prime importance. "You see, it needs to look like this, like a camel's hump. Not flat against your head," a younger woman demonstrated the finer points of hair do's and dont's.

For that brief moment, on an August afternoon, we were women together, just being women. It felt like a gate had opened and we all sat in the green meadow of Eden's unity, a tea party arranged by God.

We compared and chatted and pointed and laughed until it was time to leave. We put our shoes on, kissed each other once on the left cheek and five on the right.

We left the house filled with more than figs and tea.

31

Tables in the Wilderness

If we have no peace, it is because we have
forgotten that we belong to each other.

Mother Theresa

THE FADED, weathered relief tents were immaculately clean in the middle of the desert. This was quite a feat considering the amount of sand trudged in via feet and wind.

The rugs provided a place to sit as we waited for evening prayers to finish. We left the busy city and moved closer to the border to visit a family who remained in the desert, alone, away from the camps.

Once housed in the refugee camp, they experienced such trauma and disease that they packed up and sought refuge in the harsh desert, living in tents with only a hole in the ground for a bathroom. They served us hot tea, flavored with mint.

The men sat with us and did most of the talking. The women

looked at us and smiled warmly, speaking in Arabic. We nodded back and waited patiently for the translation.

I brought coloring pages and new crayons. I didn't know why, but on our way to visit, I grabbed a handful of photocopied papers and stuffed them into my bag. They were mostly Disney princesses. I was glad I did this as they were surprisingly wildly popular, even with the adults.

One sweet little girl took it upon herself to teach me everyone's name in Arabic. She painstakingly wrote out my name and then translated it while her mom colored Beauty and the Beast.

The whole family fled Syria in the middle of the night - all 28 men, women and children. One of the men produced a phone with videos on it.

"He wants to know if you want to see videos of their home in Syria before it was bombed," said our translator.

Yes, of course, we did. He nodded and sent his phone around the circle to us. There was a queen-sized bed with an ornately carved wooden headboard, a beautiful bedroom suite. The video continued and I winced at what was left of the bedroom, the house, the walls, the car. They saw my reaction and seemed to approve and nodded in agreement.

I kept thinking about the older man's offer. "He wants to know if you want to see…" If was honest, I didn't really want to see it. No, no I didn't. Not this close, not when I could put a face and name with the devastation and loss. It would be a lot easier to live with a blind spot and never know the pain that lurked in the unknowing.

"We left Syria. But there, in the camps, there are so many

diseases. We left the camp. Now, we have no electricity, no water, no toilet, but we don't have diseases. I would rather risk going back to Syria to be killed than to die of a disease, alone, with nothing," the older man said.

That the choice even had to be made sat in my throat, indigestible. I was sitting in the lesser of two evils. They chose to live alone in the desert with a future wrapped in dusty floor rugs and stray goats where a fleeting glimmer of hope was caked with coarse desert sand.

By the time the sun began to set, we stood to leave. The women hugged us tightly and whispered goodbyes. The children followed us to the car. I left the crayons and coloring pages with my new spelling teacher, who was now beaming and waving like a princess.

32

Dorich

If we couldn't laugh, we would all go insane.

Robert Frost

I KNEW they were laughing at me. I left the room to make some tea and I could hear the voices through the doorway speaking about me.

"Something in Arabic … Christina ... laugher ... dorich … hahaha." And it made me smile.

The day before, I sat on a floor in a circle of women, sipping hot tea and eating even more popcorn. This seemed to be the snack of choice. This time there were no kids and babies. It was more of a formal learning environment than a casual get together.

All shoes were left at the front door and we tucked our bare, dusty feet under our legs and sat cross-legged on the floor. There were at least twelve of us crammed into the small, cement house with no air conditioning in the middle of summer.

I don't understand Arabic apart from the usual greeting, As-salāmu 'alaykum, and wa'alaykum salaam and shukran, of course. When in doubt, use shukran. That was my motto.

As we sat barefoot on the floor, the women spoke in turns around the circle and each one said her name. I tried in vain to remember each name, but my usual mnemonic devices were useless as each woman was identically dressed in all black, some with only eyes showing.

My name was easy for them to remember, as was my face since I was the only white lady with frizzy blonde hair in the mix. I liked the way they said my name, with a thousand rolling r's...Chrrrrrristina. The lady next to me was Maralena.

At least that's what I kept calling her when we spoke. She and her four young daughters fled Syria at the start of the war. They were caught and put in jail. She tried to flee again and finally was successful.

She had a way of welcoming me into her space with kind, round, brown eyes, and a round face. She leaned into me as if she was telling me a secret, but she didn't say anything with words.

She didn't speak English but I felt like we had whole conversations. The lady next to her was called Dorich. She was pregnant with her fifth child and had the most regal bone structure I'd ever seen.

When I asked her a question, I called her Dorich because it was one of the few names that I could manage to retain. I was pretty proud of myself for remembering these few names so I used them liberally like a Dale Carnegie fangirl.

Later, as we shared around the circle, the translator pointed to Maralena and said, "Dorich, can you tell us what Allah has taught you this week?"

Horrified that I'd been using the wrong name, I whispered to our translator, "Wait, I thought her name was Maralena!"

"It is."

"Then why did you call her Dorich? I thought she (subtly gesturing to the regal pregnant lady) was Dorich."

Pause. Confused face.

"Hahahaha!" Clearly, the translator was having a good chuckle at my expense. Oh, ok. I loved nothing more than being a cultural pariah in front of a live audience. My long-repressed middle school shame came flooding back.

We'd been sitting cross-legged in the hot room for so long, the backs of my knees were sweaty. I squeaked when I tried to adjust myself.

Then, I heard, "Christina ... Dorich ... hahahaha...haha-hahahaha."

"No, her name is not Dorich. Dorich means 'next' so when we were going around the circle, sometimes we were saying 'dorich,' as in the next person should speak, or it was time to move to a different topic."

Oh. I see.

But it was too late. The story repeated itself over and over. I started referring to myself as Dorich, which was apparently even funnier.

The next day we met again with the same core group of women, however, every newcomer was treated to a little summary of Dorich with the blonde hair.

It was good to hear laughter. There would never be enough to balance out the war stories, but it was something. It was something that wasn't there before.

33

Not Fit For Interrogation

I imagine one of the real reasons people cling
to their hates so stubbornly is because they
sense, once hate is gone, they will be
forced to deal with the pain.

James Baldwin

I WONDERED if this little girl had ever seen snow since she lives in the hot, arid desert of Palestine. It was 10 p.m. and the kids were not remotely ready for bed.

I was standing in the middle of her kitchen. A four-year-old girl with black hair braided down the middle of her back was wearing a pink tutu while watching the Disney movie, *Frozen*. Elsa was inquiring if Anna would like to build a snowman.

The younger girl slept peacefully next to her mom, Salome, who sat on the couch slowly sipping tea, staring at the TV screen. Packets of half-eaten potato chips scattered the room.

Plastic sippy cups tipped upside down on the carpet, dropped by little hands who discovered better things to do.

The couples' wedding picture hung on the cement wall, front, and center, in a large wooden frame. He was a bit older than her; they made a striking couple dressed in white linen against olive skin, dark hair, and dark eyes.

We were introduced. Salome spoke little English, so our mutual friend translated for us when words had to be used. This night, few words were necessary. We moved slowly and quietly, matching the comatose feeling that hung in the air. It felt like we were tip-toeing around a wounded animal, trying not to disturb the pain-no sudden movements, no loud noises.

My friend Shelly and I were here for one reason: to take care of the kids. I don't speak Arabic, but I d speak baby. Salome had received a call that no mother wanted to hear. Her 21-year old son had been killed. He lived in the next town. No details were forthcoming, just the devastating call.

Her husband was en route to the morgue to identify the body. She just needed help with the kids because they were estranged from her family and they had no friends nearby. Could we help? Of course, we went.

We walked down the dark alley in the West Bank to a gray concrete apartment building not far from where we were staying. Interestingly, I felt much safer being outside there at night than in Cape Town.

Upon entering, she asked if we would like some tea as she prepared the gas stove to boil water. We all watched while she fiddled with a box of matches, dropping one and then the other until the flame connected. We sat in dread silence.

The good thing about not speaking Arabic was that I couldn't offer shallow words of consolation, which I would normally try to do out of sheer nervousness. We could only sit in the in-between, the air of death and disbelief weaving around us. The unspoken pain saturated every corner of the house.

The young girl often glanced at us, removed herself from Elsa's world and climbed into Salome's lap for brief moments to stare at us. As Salome began to talk to our friend in Arabic, I made myself useful and convinced the little girl to exchange her tutu for pajamas.

We played a few games, communicating with sign language and facial expressions as I wrapped two little girls into a thin, coarse blanket, their big brown eyes staring at me like we were all dreaming.

As soon as they started to give in to sleep, one jolted the other awake, as if they needed to show us that they were still alive. The adults sat in the lounge area, waiting. For what, I didn't know.

Like an alarm clock ringing us out of a deep sleep, a cell phone rang. Salome grabbed for her phone underneath a pile of blankets on the couch and quickly answered.

"What? How did they find out?" she barked in a voice more incredulous than mournful. She was speaking English now, more for our benefit I thought, so she didn't have to repeat the same story. She sat down, brown eyes darting between the three of us. Instead of a voice of grief, her voice suddenly switched to one of defiance.

She sprung from the couch, looked around the flat and started rifling through bureau drawers. The change in demeanor gave us emotional whiplash. She clicked the phone off, threw it into the couch and methodically moved from drawer to drawer, opening the desk, snatching handfuls of ribbon and cross-stitch projects before tearing posters from the walls.

Our friend and translator who initially summoned us here spoke to our distraught friend for some explanation. As she received word, she turned to us in a voice of steel and said, "They are coming, the police. They found out that this family is Christian."

"I thought Christianity is legal here," I said. Because now, of all times was a good time for semantics.

"Take everything off the wall that resembles anything Christian."

That response confirms the fact that I'm missing key information about my previously held assumption. I watched in disbelief as Salome removed her wedding photo from the wall.

Wait. what?

Who was coming?

The police?

What kind of police?

To do what, raid the house?

I was asking these questions in my head but I was sure they were written all over my shocked face because our friend said, "It's not illegal to be a Christian if they are *born* Christian..." She stared at me with her eyebrows raised, hoping I would connect the dots. Dots connected.

"Here, go through this photo album and take out any pictures with a cross or church in them."

I was one hundred percent certain that my adrenalin levels had never, ever skyrocketed quite like that. I was quickly flipping through family memories, peeling pictures of precious family moments from between plastic sheets of a sticky scrapbook just because they look Christian or churchy. When that was done, they handed me a pillowcase.

"Here, put things in here. Now, look at the videos and bookshelves. But arrange the shelves so that it doesn't look like things are missing or have been moved."

I stared at the shelf of videos. *Dear Lord, were Veggie Tales incriminating?* I threw Larry and Bob into the pillowcase, comparing this moment to the many moments I had spent with my own kids watching Veggie Tales snuggled on the couch without fear, panic and an irrational heart rate.

I watched Salome as she flipped open the laptop and proceeded to log into Facebook.

"I'm deleting my account," she said, her hands shaking.

"Just put the whole computer into the pillowcase. That will take too long," said our friend, like this was not the first time she'd done this.

"Hide everything that looks Christian," the plea was repeated.

I removed Joyce Meyer books, children's coloring books about Noah's ark, and a small wall calendar with Bible verses on it.

Wait a minute. Hide everything that looked Christian? I was a

165

Christian! If the police showed up here and interrogated me, I would squeal like a pig! I was the most damning evidence there! I was a mom of five kids who pretended to homeschool! I was not trained for this!

I don't think I ever, in my life, felt this level of fear. I could very easily have wet my pants. I wanted to go home. I wanted my mom.

"Maybe we shouldn't be found here," I offered, knowing that I was the weakest link. I kept praying that the phone call was a cruel hoax, an intimidation tactic and the police would not bother this grieving family.

"Not yet. Take as much as you can."

I distinctly remember Shelly looking at me saying, "Pray the police don't even bother to come tonight."

You didn't have to tell me twice.

I continued to search and removed sentimental things tucked away in books or displayed on bookshelves. We stopped for a minute to see what we'd done. There was nothing left.

We gathered the family's belongings and deeply-loved memories, crammed into a pillowcase. We took a deep breath, hugged goodbye and disappeared into the darkness with a lifetime of evidence slung onto our backs.

We found out later the police never arrived.

34

Lamentations

If you've come to take a side, for Israel or for
Palestine, don't come back. You will leave
us in pieces. But if you come to love Jews,
Muslims, and Christians, and to learn
about the situation, you are welcome
because you bring peace.

Elias Chacour

THE DAY after the incident with Salome, which incidentally
was the most harrowing moment in my life, I proposed
another wild idea to my traveling companion. Yes,
we had just encountered what sounds like something from a
Hollywood movie script. Secret police, hiding Bibles, wiping
computers and running down the road in the middle of the
night could all be officially checked off my bucket list.

Every night after our arrival, around 10:30 or so, we heard the
riots begin anew between Palestinians and the Israeli military.

Our bedroom windows were open at night in a feeble attempt to cool down from the summer heat.

This meant not only did we get a slight breeze, but we could hear gunfire, the sound of death hanging in the stuffy air, giving it a muffled echo. Not far from us was the separation wall, the security checkpoint dividing Jerusalem and Bethlehem.

Nevertheless, the next morning, I told Shelly that I had an overwhelming desire to stand in the physical place of conflict. She promptly declined because she has a rational head and an astute mind. I was, however, convinced that this was what I needed to do. Our heart rates had barely lowered since last night's adrenaline rush, but Shelly eventually agreed to come with me.

We slipped on our sensible shoes and began walking from our house through the city of Bethlehem toward the separation wall. We walked past the refugee camps with white gravel in the yard instead of grass, past green faded couches sitting in vacant lots, upholstery stuffing bursting from the cushion, past twisted, rusted barbed wire fences, past a posh hotel with valets in stiff jackets covered in gold buttons, past storefronts and grocery markets with the sales of the week plastered to glass windows.

As we got closer to the wall, we could smell it - skunk water. The putrid stench was used by Israeli Defense Forces to dispel crowds. Shot from water cannons, the spray soaked into clothes, surged through open windows, drenched furniture and induced a gag reflex like no one's business.

Palestinians who have been sprayed described it as "worse

than raw sewage" and "like a mixture of excrement, noxious gas, and a decomposing donkey."

Despite the attempts to sanitize the streets, the sewage mixture left us no choice but to walk with our scarves over our noses, trying to breathe through our mouths. We walked through neighborhoods and streets with kids playing ball games and businesses buzzing until suddenly, there it was.

This huge, grey, hulking wall with a militarized checkpoint rose out of the neighborhood. It was a 400-mile wall built within the occupied Palestinian territories. In the area in which I was standing, the wall rose at least 20-feet, the joints held together by circular towers of armed guards, overlooking the area. Graffiti artwork covered the wall, the Israeli military on one side and the marks of resistance on the other.

This was where I lost it. As soon as I stepped into its shadow, I couldn't breathe. I nearly doubled over from the pain in my stomach. The tears wouldn't stop and the words wouldn't come. It was the first time in my life I felt someone's pain so deeply.

I began praying from deep within my gut, only in phrases, aware that we had to keep walking in order to avoid suspicion from the armed guards above us.

The more I prayed for truth and love to live there, the better I felt until eventually, the heaviness subsided. Shelly told me that this was true lament, when you feel so deeply for someone else, you grieve on their behalf. It felt like birth pains.

We left the wall and walked through the checkpoint amidst the military blockade and found our bus headed into

Jerusalem. After miles and miles of walking, we found ourselves standing in front of the Knesset, Israel's parliament in Jerusalem.

The neatly manicured lawn was green and lush, a rose garden sat next to the building, with trees that provided shade covering to families sitting on the grass, food and blanket spread before them.

Shelly wanted to walk around the building and pray for the government inside, but the entrance guard stopped us. He had a big gun, so we felt compelled to stop. We asked if we could just walk around the building. He surprised us and asked if we wanted to go *inside* and sit in a session. *Wait, what? We could go inside?*

After a series of security measures, we were escorted into the balcony section where we sat behind a sheet of fiberglass and overlooked the parliamentarians while they debated something. It looked important.

Within a matter of minutes, they were clearly voting, hands raised in various motions. It was all in Hebrew but numbers flashed on an electronic scoreboard like a basketball game, indicating that someone had indeed won.

The whole time we sat in there we prayed for the government. It felt like we were in an invisible bubble. No one paid any attention to us.

My heart became so heavy for this country living in such fear. What a nation, what a history, and here I was, watching the policies of the future unfold before me. I imagined the resilience of this nation as I sat in awe. This prayer session was much less emotional, yet just as powerful.

As quickly as we got in, we both had the sense it was time to leave. For the first time that day, I felt an overwhelming sense of peace that each side of this conflict had been upheld in prayer.

We grabbed shawarma from a street vendor for dinner and went to bed pretty early; that kind of emotion takes a toll.

I don't pretend to know why. Looking back, I can't believe I did it. But I knew, deep inside my spirit, that I had to do it. Up until this trip, I can't remember ever praying as intensely as I did then.

I have been praying in more ways than I ever thought possible these last few years. I now know that we don't need to use our own language or verbalized words which often serves to transport our own agenda.

I've learned that prayer is embodied, not just cognitive. It is feeling the heart of God for a person, place or situation and choosing to be the carrier of light, regardless of the outcome or benefit to me.

Sometimes, it means disrupting the negative atmosphere and infusing it with Love itself. If the Kingdom of God is within me, I don't need to distribute gospel tracts on the street corner to make a difference. I can choose to radiate from the inside what needs to be present on the outside.

Two weeks after we returned to South Africa, I read the news. Israel and Gaza had signed a ceasefire agreement. Do I believe our prayers played a small part in that? Yes, yes I do. There are many, many intercessors praying on behalf of the Israelis and Palestinians.

But for those few weeks, during that tense summer, I was there. I physically felt the pain of the conflict in my body and I imagined a place filled with hope.

35

Lessons from the Bus

Love sometimes wants to do us a great favor-
Hold us upside down and shake all the
nonsense out.

Hafez

AFTER OUR TIME in Jordan and our death-defying experience with the police, Shelly and I decided we needed a break
from the sirens, bomb warnings, and unrest. I have profound
respect for people who live there however, we had to get
away from the chaos to save our sanity.

At night, we were lulled to sleep with the sound of guns, air
sirens and the endless buzzing from my stupid phone. I
mistakenly thought it would be a good idea to install an app
that alerted me to nearby missile strikes. Yes indeed, I got a
notification every time there was a missile attack. I don't
know how I went from having the Krispy Kreme "Hot and
Now" app to a missile notification app, but I did. Both were
hazardous to my health.

Shelly discovered a delightful hostel online with a vacancy in the northern, coastal city of Haifa. It was on this 'holiday' of sorts that I was about to continue my string of cultural mishaps. We chose Haifa, in part, because of the coast, but also because according to my "Hot and Now" missile detection app, Haifa looked like it was out of range so maybe our sleep-deprived selves could get some peace and quiet.

We packed lightly, carrying just duffle bags and backpacks and set out in the direction of the separation wall and checkpoint to connect to our party bus. As we neared the checkpoint, I pulled out my passport with the accompanying Israeli visa, which was required documentation going into Jerusalem from that side of the wall. There were soldiers who would soon board our bus to check our documentation, at gunpoint.

From my window seat, I saw the most fascinating scene. A young, striking Israeli soldier with high cheekbones, and dark, curly hair secured at the back of her head, boarded our bus. She couldn't be more than 18-years-old. She climbed up the steps into the bus, shifting a large, menacing gun from one shoulder to another.

Before she began the descent down the aisle, she flipped down the bus visor, peering into the mirror as she ran her finger over her lips smoothing brightly colored lipstick.

Without thinking, I whipped out my cell phone and took a picture of this fascinating hybrid of little girl and armed soldier. This was before the days I learned to be inconspicuous with my hot pink Otter box. I thought nothing of it as she suddenly disembarked.

Another stern-looking guy took her place and walked from seat to seat, examining passports. As I continued to stare out my window, I could see my fascinating soldier talking excitedly to a circle of other soldiers. Was it just my imagination or was she gesturing at me? No, it couldn't be. I had my documentation.

The Arab bus driver made some sort of an announcement. I don't speak Arabic so I ignored it, which is not the best foreign relations policy. That was when I felt the eyes of the bus turn toward me. *Wait, was he speaking English now? Was he talking to me? But why?* He was definitely making eye contact with me.

"You!" He gestured excitedly to get off the bus, extending his arm and finger to the door.

"Me?" I gestured back, most definitely not excitedly.

"Yes, you." Um ok, yeah so I was going to get off the bus and apparently disappear. I hoped Shelly was watching and was prepared to call the US embassy to explain my kidnapping. I glanced back to see if she noticed the commotion. She did not. She was looking at her phone.

Oh no, was this about the picture? It had to be the picture. I grabbed my phone with the hot pink case and nonchalantly attempted to remove the sim card with one hand while looking calm on the outside. Like, seriously, who was I? Jason Bourne? How was I going to delete that photo in the space of the ten meters that I had to walk off this bus to where a circle of the Israeli Defense Force awaited my presence?

Too late. I was descending the stairs and approaching the circle. "Hey, what's up," I asked, making my eyes as wide and innocent as I could manage.

HEY, WHAT'S UP? Did I just whazzzzupp the IDF? Was this my default behavior in crisis? Dear Lord, I am obnoxious! Please God, tell me I didn't just saunter as I approached. I think I sauntered. My hands were in my pockets all causal like I was waltzing into a hipster café, Moleskin under my arm.

The young girl emerged from the circle with her gun pointed in my direction. It was not directed at me, but it was not like it was hiding. I mentally admired her choice of fuchsia tinted lipstick. It looked divine with her olive complexion.

"Which bag is yours?" she asked while gesturing at the storage space underneath the bus. It had been opened and several dogs were sniffing around the space. At least I got to take my belongings with me to prison. I hate leaving my contacts in overnight.

"That one there," I pointed. "With the Union Jack on the side."

"What's that?" she barked.

"The British flag in pink floral." *For the love of Pete, why was I being so descriptive?* She removed the bag from the bus. The dog on a leash sniffed it with an air of condescension.

"Open it."

I opened the bag and she probed inside, finding nothing but some plus size capri pants, toiletries, and my journal. She zipped it again and put it back under the bus.

"Ok. You're fine." She motioned for me to get back on the bus.

Oh my word, that was it? I boarded the bus and sat back down. Shelly still hadn't noticed. A toothless, old lady across from me was grinning while clutching her cane. If I wasn't mistaken, she was laughing at me. I settled into my bus ride and decompressed as our bus sped toward Haifa.

ONCE THERE, we walked an unreasonable distance uphill to locate our hostel in the midst of lush greenery, not far from the Baha'i Gardens on Mount Carmel. The owner of the hostel, a happy, German chap in his mid-forties with tanned skin and buzzed, blonde hair, gave us a tour of the place, nonchalantly pointing out that the kitchen was as good a place as any to retreat to as a bomb shelter.

I thought maybe he was being sarcastic because quite frankly, the kitchen is always my go-to place in a crisis. He wasn't joking. Indeed, someone had taped a sign with the words *Bomb Shelter* in comic sans above the teacups.

Shelly and I had the 12-bunk room to ourselves for which I was extremely grateful. We scanned the local list of things to do in Haifa and decided that a nice meal on the boardwalk sounded like an excellent plan. Haifa didn't appear to have as many English speakers as Jerusalem. There was both Hebrew and Arabic, but not so much English. We followed some choppy directions and eventually arrived at a bus stop.

To find my way around Haifa, (my South African sim card was not useful in foreign lands) I resorted to taking screen-shots of the MapQuest directions in Hebrew and then walking around the street aimlessly, showing my cell phone photos to someone who could translate them into English. There was no dignity left in me, but I got where I wanted to go.

Despite the dark night, people were bustling and city lights were twinkling, giving the city a golden glow against the pitch black night, such a contrast to the border chaos we left behind.

At the bus stop, we met a friendly Palestinian lady who spoke English and generously gave us restaurant recommendations on the boardwalk. Since we were both traveling in the same direction, she boarded the bus with us.

She sat across the aisle and announced that at the next stop her mom would board and her young kids would be in tow. She was an optometrist and her mom cared for her kids after school.

When an elderly lady in a tracksuit boarded with two school aged-children in uniforms, she introduced us to each one like we'd been lifelong friends instead of friends since stop 21.

We chatted a bit about where we were from, what we were doing in Haifa and so on. Shelly and I explained that we lived in South Africa and we are in Haifa on holiday, which was mostly true. We certainly didn't want to get anyone in trouble and I'd learned that you never knew who was watching you around there.

"Oh," she exclaimed, "I'd love to visit South Africa someday and take my kids to see it. I would love that but from what I hear, it's just too dangerous of a place."

I stared at her and for a full second. I couldn't decide if she had superior sarcasm skills or if she was genuinely afraid to visit South Africa. Granted, South Africa's reputation for crime was both well deserved and widespread. But there were bombs and war and guns in Israel which to me was infinitely more frightening.

I was certain my face registered the irony because she said, "You know, we are used to *this*, with a wave of her hand. We grew up with it. But *that* would be a different type of danger. We don't know of *that* type."

It is true. We are conditioned to accept a certain lifestyle as our normal. Until you visit a place and speak to the people, you just don't know what you don't know.

And she doesn't know what she was missing.

36

Kittens, Kevin and Kommetjie Road

Normality is a paved road: It's comfortable to
walk, but no flowers grow on it.

Vincent van Gogh

I HAD BEEN BACK in South Africa for a few months,
adjusting to life as normal. By normal, I mean without the
bombs and tear gas that I got to experience from my expedi-
tions in the Middle East.

Our cat, Wookie, gave birth to kittens a few weeks before my
return. The day arrived when we loaded the furry little guys
into the car for their first trip to the veterinarian.

We had a new-to-us-car. It was fancy, a 1997 Volvo automatic
with somewhat leather seats. It floated down the road like a
grandma's ride to church. It was just missing the smell of
Juicy Fruit and the palpable anticipation of lunch at an all-
you-can-eat-buffet.

We barely pulled the car out of our driveway when the weird

engine sound started. Kevin drove on bravely despite the fact that I was yelling about a strange noise. He carried on like he heard nothing. He wouldn't even make eye contact, his denial was so deep.

The Volvo escalated its temper tantrum until finally, like a father of toddlers who wouldn't behave, Kevin scowled, sighed and yanked the steering wheel, directing the car to the side of the very busy main road.

There was a weird pile of metal shavings on the road. I was holding a box of kittens.

The thing was that we were on Kommetjie Road, the main road that everyone drove every day, all the time. Seeing us with car problems was not out of the ordinary. Indeed, one friend drove by, honked their horn and gave a jovial wave as they whizzed by us. I swore they accelerated. No one dared come to our rescue lest they fall under the same automotive curse.

The kittens were restless. Little paws reached for me in between a wire mesh covering.

I decided to get out of the car. I hoisted the squealing box from the car, trying to soothe the little piles of fluff and not looking like a crazy cat lady.

Yes, it was me, just sitting on the side of the road talking to a box of kittens. Carry on.

Kevin was now underneath the car, inspecting. A friend of ours, Marty, came to our rescue. She wore a yellow safety vest. I bet she carried a safety vest and flares in her car at all times for occasions such as this. These are good types of friends to have.

She started directing traffic away from Kevin's torso, which was now precariously under the car, while only his legs poked out from underneath. She scolded a taxi named Sexyli-cious as it sped past us, unaware.

I was sitting on the side of the road with a box of kittens.

We had to call for help. I made Kevin ask the tow truck driver if he would stop at the vet before dropping the car at the mechanic. Kittens first, car second.

He agreed.

We all loaded into the tow truck, Kevin, me and a box of kittens.

It was good to be back to normal.

37

Don't Throw a Cat in My Face

> If I claim to be an ally of a person or a group
> of people and I am not getting hit by the
> stones thrown at them then I am not
> standing close enough.
>
> Stan Mitchell

OUTSIDE ON OUR FRONT PORCH, we stood, paused in painful time. The chilly, winter Cape Town wind whirled around us. The cumbersome taxis whizzed by, horns sounding on the busy street. Groups of two or three people huddled together, waiting at the bus stop, shouting and laughing, unknowing.

My friend had just received a terrible phone call, carrying the dreadful news of her father's fatal car accident. She came to tell me but didn't make the final steps inside the house.

We stood on the front porch swelling with terror and emotion. She hung onto me and I held her in my arms. She is living here in Cape Town, her family in Zimbabwe. It would take a 22-hour bus ride just to reach her family.

Grief demanded expression and I was not raised to show such. She, in her African skin, was no stranger to expression and is boldly free with unrestrained emotion. I, in my awkward skin, was unsettled at the expression and depth of pain that stood between us. I didn't know what to do with this, this heaviness, this audible lament.

For a while, I just stood still. I wondered if anyone else could hear her wailing. Out of the corner of my eye, I saw small children in uniforms walking home from school, their world still intact. I was caught in the in-between of mortality and innocence.

I mentally ran through a checklist of what I should say to bring comfort in this situation even though I fully knew better than to attempt something so superficial.

Yet, I did not like the presence of suffering and on a selfish level, I was ready for it to disappear. What could I possibly offer her to stem the tide of tears?

Oddly, I landed on, "Would you like a cat?"

One of our new kittens skittered through the garden and it caught my eye. Of all the things to say, I was pretty sure she wasn't expecting that. She unwound herself from me and stared in disbelief as if she was not sure she heard right. Unfortunately, she heard right.

"No, I don't want your cat." Ok, that was understandable. I didn't really want the cat right then either.

I had never been good at the emotional exchange thing. In a

traumatic situation? Forget it, no one should come near me unless you want a domestic animal.

At the shift of emotional tide, we walked into the house where I made us tea and we sat on the couch and spoke of the surreal and planned for the unthinkable.

That got me thinking...how had I been conditioned to grieve? Had I ever sat with someone in deep, speechless lament? It wasn't really part of my American upbringing. In fact, I didn't know many people who were taught how to grieve or how to let others grieve.

My friend knew how to grieve healthfully. The art of lament was a life lesson in a society where grief was commonplace. It was necessary for survival.

For me, a Westerner with reserved emotions, this was uncomfortable, bearing witness to the presence of pain. I wanted to make it stop, get past this, jump in and save them. I wanted to skip over the teeming pool of pain to get to the healing on the other side.

In fact, I tried to take a flying jump over it, hoping to land in the happily ever-after instead of trudging knee-deep into the unknown, risking the undercurrent of mutual pain.

In the presence of an emotional connection, my defense mechanism was to throw in a cat. When I did that, I built a wall between us. I created more violence when I granted my place of comfort more privilege than that of pain.

LOOKING BACK at this life lesson, I can see where

expressing grief and lament was a missing component in my life.

A friend recently posted on social media the devastating news about a friend of hers who suddenly died at age 47, and how she was terribly distraught. I responded with a sad emoji. It wasn't even words, just an animated expression with a fat, yellow head of what I might have said if I had been there in person.

When we turn away from grief, we diminish the other and disqualify their fear, anger, and sadness. It's the equivalent of putting a cat in my face. The emotion of it all can't be contained with logic or enlightenment. It can't be squelched with a cerebral reckoning. It is alive, this emotion, and looking for a safe place to land.

I have grown in this area. I have learned. It was one of the many things that Africa taught me so well, so gently. If we can't connect with ourselves, and our deepest emotions, we can't connect with each other.

Reconciliation with each other begins with reconciliation to ourselves.

38

Another One Bites the Dust

And the King will answer them, "Don't you
know? When you cared for one of the least
important of these my little ones, my true
brothers and sisters, you demonstrated love
for me."

Jesus

EVERY THREE YEARS we must re-apply for a visa to
continue to live in South Africa. The process demanded that
we return to America to re-apply in person at the South
African Embassy in Chicago. The process also required
health physicals, a tuberculosis x-ray, which was quite an
inquisitive endeavor, fingerprinting and FBI checks.

We couldn't mail in the application, it had to be submitted in
person between the morning hours of 8-12 on a weekday. No
appointments were given. If there was no time allotted for us,
we had to return the next day which meant another hotel stay
until we could be seen.

It was no easy mission, I could tell you that. We raised money for seven flights back to America for an 8-week visit that took us around the country in a whirlwind of visitations and reunions.

Do you know what else was fun about returning to the US ? We no longer had a place to live or a car to drive. Thankfully, family members and friends opened their homes to us and we hopped around the country driving borrowed cars.

We were so grateful for the people in our lives who said, "Oh hey, I've got an extra car. Why don't you just drive it for like eight weeks?" A sweet friend lent us a van to drive from Ohio to Texas and back again. It was no ordinary van. It was a team van-a 15-seater. It either belonged to a church youth group or a homeschooling family.

After driving from Ohio to Texas, with a stop in Kansas, we prepared to make the trek back to Ohio. We left my sister Hollie's house in Dallas at 11 p.m. The air conditioning in the van wasn't working so we thought we'd rather drive through the cooler part of the night than drive through the Texas summer like a Hot Pocket on wheels.

We had been driving 13-hours straight when it happened. While coasting through southern Illinois there was all at once a loud hissing, shrieking, and grumbling. That was just me.

Then the van made a weird noise that caused us all to cringe in horror. It stopped and refused to go any further than the side of Interstate 57 in the middle of nowhere. N.O.W.H.E.R.E. It was shortly after noon on a hot, summer day.

Roadside assistance was of no assistance whatsoever. The tow truck company said they would send someone for us in two to three hours. So we waited. All five kids tumbled out, spread a sleeping bag on the side of the highway and set up some card games.

There was precious little space between the highway berm and the ditch. We had no water except the half-used water bottles we found rolling around on the floor of the van. The woods were our special lavatory.

I called my dad who called his motorcycle gang in hopes of utilizing the biker gang network to locate someone nearby who could help. Bikers always come to the rescue. The fact that my parents belonged to a motorcycle gang should be recorded as normal grandparent-like behavior. If your grandma doesn't bedazzle her Harley, do you even have a grandma?

LESSON: Next time I see what looks like a home school convention on the side of a major interstate, I will at least stop and offer some water or an educational game. We lolled around on the side of the road while semi trucks whizzed by creating a celebrated breeze, yet gently massaging us with gravel pellets.

Finally, the tow truck driver appeared, confirming my fear. He had enough room in his truck to take the team van and one person back to civilization. Why didn't they make family-sized tow truck cabs with a mini bar? Here was the pickle - he said it was illegal to leave people stranded on the side of the road while towing their vehicle.

I was not great at math but if you had only enough space for one person, and there were seven of us here, that left six of us without a place to go. We are literally six people sitting on the side of the road with nothing but a gas station in a 10-mile radius. I was not so sure about this "no one left behind law" since there seemed to be some glitches in its execution.

I was prepared to hitchhike into the next town because after 13 hours in the van and five weeks of eating Krispy Kreme, I needed some exercise. But noooo....couldn't do that because of "the law" about leaving people stranded.

That brought us to our next option, "the hide-away" option. The tow truck driver proposed we ride IN THE VAN WHILE IT WAS ON THE TOW TRUCK BED. I was not sure this was legal either, especially since he told us to keep our heads down.

Kevin sat in the truck's cab while the five kids and I scaled the side of the tow truck and tumbled into the van which was now balancing on the tow truck bed, held in place by chains. We each tucked in so that our heads couldn't be seen from the road. If you've ever wanted to know what it was like to ride in a car while being towed, it is pretty awesome. There were shrieks of delight, even some selfies.

The tow truck driver did not want to be seen driving his illegal cargo, and we would certainly raise suspicion if he drove into a populated area and then we poured out of the van, so he smuggled us into an RV campground. That's right.

He didn't just drop us off at the entrance of the park and bid us adieu. Oh no, he drove and drove into the bowels of a trailer park in the nether regions of Illinois.

Upon seeing that we were headed well away from the interstate and into a dark forest littered with Budweiser cans, one kid yelled, "This is it, we are going to die like this." He might not be wrong.

Instead of a scene from CSI, he dropped us off near a campsite with benches and a fire pit. How did he know this was here? Did he live here? Did he spend his weekends playing corn hole here? I was quite unsure of the next plan of action as we were deposited into this backwoods trailer park. Kevin, the tow truck and the van all disappeared from sight.

Ok, this was fine, just fine, I thought. There was nothing that could go wrong with any of this. At least there were people in the campground. A lady was throwing a bucket of water over the stair railing of her trailer, eyeing us suspiciously.

This place was much better than the side of the interstate, however, it felt a bit awkward like we were the newcomers in the crowd, which we were. Maybe the residents were accustomed to tow trucks dropping loads of people here. What if those families never left and they were just absorbed into the trailer park?

Meanwhile, from a distance, my dad found a local church who owned a church bus of sorts and they volunteered to help us. They must have belonged to the underground biker network. Within 15 minutes, a medium sized bus pulled up next to us in the woods with the words The First Baptist Church painted on the side.

The town where the van was towed had a Subway which was good for a 6-inch meatball sub, but didn't have much else. We picked Kevin up at the mechanic's garage and the church bus then drove us to the next town where there was a chain of three-star hotels from which to choose. There was some event going on in town and there was one room available. We took it for $179 per night.

After not sleeping the night before, sitting in the hot sun, and smuggling ourselves into a trailer park, we finally had a good night's sleep in a hotel with free breakfast. The church bus driver, Dale, left us with an invitation to stay with his family, should we need another place to stay. How very kind, I thought and took his cell phone number to be polite. Surely, our borrowed van would be on the road in no time. We could tolerate a night in the Best Western.

Just before our checkout time, we got a call from the mechanic who delivered disturbing news. His initial estimate was $800-$1200 and he would look at it that day but there was a possibility that he wouldn't be able to get the parts until Monday.

Monday?! That was two more days of us sleeping in a hotel and eating at Subway! The van repair bill and the costly hotels would soon deplete the bank account. This couldn't be real, I thought. Did car problems just follow us around the globe? Surely, he could get it fixed that day. This is America, after all.

After a few tense conversations, a bout of denial mixed with tears and gnashing of teeth, I suddenly remembered the friendly invitation from the church bus driver. I didn't know what possessed me to do it, but I called him. I called a complete stranger and said that our stay in Marion, Illinois, was going to take longer than expected.

There was something so kind and gentle about this man. He was open and honest and fatherly from the moment he opened those hydraulic church bus doors.

I didn't even know what I was going to say if he picked up the phone, which he did.

"Hi Dale, this is Christina. You picked us up on the side of the road, remember?"

"Yes, yes I remember. What's the latest news with the van?"

"It looks like tomorrow or Monday will be the soonest they can get a part for it. But we are hopeful for today."

"Ok. We've got room for you all. I've already spoken with my wife. We have a guest bedroom and a furnished basement for the kids to sleep. We have a freezer full of food and Leanne is stopping for dinner on the way home from work. I can finish up at work here and come to pick you up at your hotel."

PAUSE HERE FOR DRAMATIC EFFECT. YES, COMPLETE STRANGERS INVITED US TO STAY IN THEIR HOME.

I was hoping that he and his wife would maybe invite us for dinner so I could stop feeding the kids gas station hot dogs. I honestly couldn't believe there were people this generous in the world.

Look, at that point, we basically had no choice.

We could not afford to stay in a hotel.

We could not abandon the borrowed van.

We were hours from a bus station or anything transportation related.

This was our only option. I felt strangely…safe.

We arrived at Dale and Leanne's home and they immediately gave us a tour of the house, inviting us into their spacious country home. It was a ranch-style with a vegetable garden and an outdoor basketball hoop, complete with decorative yard animals.

Rabbits, squirrels, and geese made of stone stoically peered at us from beds of pine nugget mulch beds. Either this was Narnia and we'd just wandered into the lair of the White Witch or this was truly Midwest hospitality. I only found out later from Dale that people were fearing for his safety because who knew what kind of homeschooling criminal masterminds he invited into his house.

Maybe we were con artists and thieves, posing as missionaries on the interstate. I mean, sure, it was plausible, although, if I was a con artist I would have fired myself. Attempting a heist in southern Illinois without a getaway vehicle was not the brightest nor most lucrative of plans.

I found the fear factor surrounding us to be insulting on many levels. At the same time, I don't think I would've picked us up on the side of the road if I were Dale.

On Sunday, Dale and Leanne invited us to go to church with them in a nearby town, which, funnily enough, was not the same church whose bus picked us up. We went to church and Dale introduced us to people as the family he found on the side of the road.

Church was nice. They offered us free coffee and pens. Afterwards, we ate lunch together at Fazzoli's which was fast food Italian with all-you-could-eat-breadsticks.

Sunday lunch after church was something my family always did together and this felt quite comfortable and familiar like we'd done it before. Had we really only known these people for a few days?

Monday rolled around and we packed and prepared to leave. Dale and Leanne both went to work, leaving a family of seven in their house with all their food. They even gave us the keys to one of their cars, should we need to run errands before we left.

Kevin awaited the phone call from the automotive shop to let us know when we could pick up the van and finish the drive home. The call arrived later in the day.

"They thought they found the part they need to repair the van but they didn't. Maybe tomorrow."

"Um, what?" That was the abbreviated version of what I said. There were more expletives. I couldn't believe it as I ran through the list of scheduled meetings we would have to cancel since we would not be making a road trip that day.

On Tuesday, we called the mechanic to no avail. I tried Facebook, messaging the business asking for an update. No response. I moved to Twitter. No amount of passive-aggressive tweeting could rile a response from that place.

Finally, at the end of the day, the mechanic called back. He hadn't had time to look at the van but there was still a few working hours left, so fingers crossed. Hopefully, tomorrow it would be fixed.

At 11:30 am on Wednesday Kevin called the shop, hoping for the best, but fearing the worst. They told him that not only was it not done, but they were waiting on another part that wasn't due to be delivered until later that day. Surely, I thought, this was a cruel joke.

No call. Dale and Leann were understanding and patient. They even asked the kids what food they would like to have in the house so they could go to the store and buy them their favorite comfort foods. Seriously, they were grandparenting gold.

One week since the tow truck driver left us in the woods the mechanic called to say it is finished. *It is finished.* We rose up out of there and hit the road like it was our job.

You know the story of the good Samaritan? We just lived through it. There were several people who could have helped us but chose to pass by on the other side of the road. There was one couple who opened their home, fed us and took care of every need we had at their own expense.

We never heard from Dale and Leanne again. But if you live in Marion, Illinois, find them and give them a big hug from us. They are the best Samaritans.

39

Thanksgiving

May your troubles be less and your blessings
be more. And nothing but happiness come
through your door.

Irish blessing

CELEBRATING Thanksgiving in South Africa has several obvious hurdles to overcome before celebrating the day.

Hurdle #1 -(and this is a surprise to some Americans) It's not an international holiday. It is just a Thursday. We worked until 5 p.m. Do you know how hard it was to work all day and then come home and whip up something Thanksgiving-y? The benefit was that stores were still open for last-minute butter runs.

Hurdle #2 -There are no big, fat turkeys. There are only little, game hen sizes. I had heard a rumor about a butcher in town who offered larger turkeys to ex-pats on this special day but could not find him. Few had ever seen him. He was probably a myth.

For a big crowd, we needed to make a lot of little turkey birds. This was a lot of work, not to mention the calculations involved in predicting how many bite-sized birds were required for a crowd. We had yet to get this right. Five years running and we had no leftovers, which was criminal. It was impossible to eat oneself into a food coma on a kiddie-sized portion of tryptophan.

Hurdle #3 -Describing the delicacy known as "stuffing" to non-Americans. My favorite definition was, "soggy bread cooked inside a turkey's butt." This didn't make non-Americans want to taste stuffing. Each year Kevin went on an adventurous rampage in search of a stuffing that sounded appetizing.

He created wild mushroom stuffing, sausage stuffing, and traditional stuffing. Each year people asked what it was and each year I hollered out my definition without hesitation. Oh well, more for me.

Hurdle #4 -Everything must be made from scratch. There is no Stove Top stuffing mix, no canned pumpkin puree for pumpkin pies, not even candy pumpkins or candy corn. This was actually not at all bad, as we cooked much healthier. But seriously, have you ever made a pumpkin pie from the actual pumpkin? I didn't even know it was a thing! For the entirety of my adult life, I assumed pumpkin pie puree just made an appearance around Thanksgiving like Peeps did on Easter.

We dried our own bread for stuffing, deep-fried onions for the topping on a green bean casserole and even had a weird relationship with cranberries. When all was said and done, a Thanksgiving meal was a five-star production. It was so flipping good. No short cuts, which was a mission because of hurdle number one.

Hurdle #5 -I wanted to use cute, autumnal decorations but alas, November is spring in South Africa. Also, no Target stores for the latest in table decor, no cute Fall decorations, no leaves changing color, no Fall inspired tablecloths. It was a morale booster when someone sent a care package that included cute fall napkins, a papier-mâché turkey and miniature, plastic pumpkins.

Once, I was able to find a few orange pumpkins but most of them were gray. Gray pumpkins. Nothing said melancholy gratitude, with a hint of nausea like a gray pumpkin centerpiece.

Hurdle #6 -No Black Friday. For reasons unbeknownst to me, South Africa has adopted a Black Friday shopping day on Friday after our Thanksgiving. They called it Black Friday, and it was on a Friday. But since they didn't celebrate Thanksgiving, it was just a random Friday in late November.

They haven't quite capture the nuances of early bird sales, or quite frankly, a good sale worth waking for at 2 a.m. on a holiday weekend. It is just weird.

Back in Ohio, I combed through the advertisements from the big, fat newspaper that came out on Thanksgiving. Mildly bulbous and sleepy from a Thanksgiving meal, half the family would watch football and nap, the smell of freshly brewed coffee mixed with a crisp chill in the air. Others sat cross-legged on the floor amid a shimmery pile of colorfully, seductive fliers from every department store in the tristate area.

Those were good times, not that I did any of that. I slept in and silently judged those who glorified the capitalistic machine, except the one year I got an iPad at a ridiculously cheap price. Still, Black Friday sales are a tradition beholden to the American psyche that was conjoined to Thanksgiving. You just can't have Black Friday without Thanksgiving.

One particular year, we went to the home of an American friend who also lived in Cape Town. She invited an eclectic bunch of internationals and a handful of Americans. We brought pumpkin pies. Ethan made a triple chocolate layered pie with an Oreo crust (from scratch) and green bean casserole.

Kevin took the day off so he voluntarily worked all day on the festive delights. I had the luxury of coming home, cleaning up, grabbing a pie and walking out the door.

On our way to Kommetjie, which is a little beach town down the road, our car acted like one of its personalities was taking over. As we pulled away from the robot (traffic light), our car unashamedly drove no faster than 20 km per hour, despite Kevin's foot adamantly on the gas pedal.

As we turned, our car decided it was done driving. We pulled off the road, realizing in horror that it was an electrical problem. Pity, we all had our windows down just before it quit. Leaving an abandoned car on the side of the road was basically an invitation for theft. It was insured, at least.

I crossed my fingers that someone would make good on the reputation of the area and steal it. It was nothing but trouble. (Spoiler alert. Nobody stole it. We just couldn't catch a break).

We sat there, not even stunned, but in a collective blasé because, of course, this would happen to us. We weren't that far from the home of sweet potatoes and stuffing so we got out of the car, pies in hand, preparing to traipse down the road like every family with four kids carrying crockpots would do.

Thankfully, a nice German friend came to our rescue in his always reliable German car. We piled in and continued on to Thanksgiving. The car repair could wait. We had a Thanksgiving feast awaiting us. We joined a handful of Americans in South Africa, to celebrate an American holiday.

Surrounding us were Germans, Kiwis, Swiss, South Africans, Americans born and raised in South Africa, a Dutch girl married to a man from the Comoros Islands, a Canadian girl raised in Columbia, married to a coloured South African. And us. Straight outta the Midwest. Thankful.

40

Brussels, Paris and a Coffee Cart

Clearly, clearly, my job here is not to go to the
town plaza and make proselytes; it is to
live wrapped in God, trembling to His
thoughts, burning with His passion. And,
my loved one, that is the best gift you can
give to your own town.

Frank Laubach

IN THE SPRING OF 2016, I found myself between two cities, Paris and Brussels, weeks after consecutive terrorist attacks had torn through both cities. For whatever reason, I am drawn to a crisis like a moth to flame.

I had traveled with a small outreach team from South Africa. We connected with an international Christian volunteer organization to see if we could help in some way.

"What will you do?" everyone asked, as if *doing something* was more important than just *being there*. I didn't know what exactly we would "do" but I didn't have grandiose ideas of being aid workers who would save the planet.

The plan was to stay in Brussels for a few weeks and then move on to Paris. As I was walked through the streets of Brussels, there was silence within silence. People were moving, cars were honking and shops were open but there was a heavy grief that sat in the eyes of people we passed.

Together, the four of us from South Africa and two local Europeans, walked through historic Jubelpark (Parc du Cinquantenaire), pulling a makeshift coffee cart, which we intended to distribute for free. The sun was shining while the winter air still taunted us, forcing us to wear both sunscreen and a jacket.

A handful of university students walked across the lawn, approaching us. They were from Brazil and spoke little English. We spoke zero Portuguese. My friend offered a cup of coffee. They smiled and began to explain that they were studying and couldn't get back home until the year was over, despite being so very afraid after the terror attacks in the subway. They hadn't ridden the subway since more than 30 people were killed by a rogue bomb at the Molenbeek stop.

A young guy in his mid-twenties was occupying a space of green lawn while sprawled on his back in the grass, expensive headphones on his ears, Ray-Ban sunglasses covering his eyes. His tank top revealed several ink murals which were wildly distorted by the contour of abnormally large biceps. *Please God, don't ask me to talk to this guy.*

I'd rather talk to the group of moms sitting on the grass with their toddlers who didn't have muscles the size of soup cans. Nevertheless, this guy was clearly drawing my attention.

Ugh, I argued with myself, no one wanted to have their zen interrupted by a stranger trying to talk over their music. Nevertheless, I listened to my gut and that still, small voice and made my way toward him.

As I approached him, he seemed only mildly irritated that a middle-aged woman with frizzy curls was blocking his sunlight and interrupting his solitude. I assumed he would turn down my offer for free coffee and that would be that. I would have assuaged the voice in my head and kept most of my dignity intact.

Here was the plan, I reasoned with myself, I'd make the offer as lame as possible and he would politely decline and I'd move on to the moms.

"Hey," I started. "We've got free coffee there if you want some." Surely, no one took up that offer. It was like taking homemade cookies from strangers. You didn't know who had laced it with arsenic.

"Pardon? Café?" he said. "Café, yes," I said and pointed to the cart where the Brazilian students were still congregating.

I covered my shock as he removed his headphones and agreed to a cup of coffee. We chatted briefly as we walked toward the coffee cart. His smile was genuine and his shoulders became less defensive, more open.

We compared tattoos and he excitedly explained the meaning behind his artwork. It was a family tattoo, just like his father's. We talked for close to an hour or so about the city, the attack and how we needed each other.

He was overcome, he said, and visibly moved that I stopped to offer him coffee and did not pass by. "Most people don't approach me in public, you know?" he said. I couldn't imagine why not.

WE PULLED our coffee cart further into the park toward the massive concrete fountain, where we parked it under shade trees. There was a group of three dark-complected men with beards standing in a circle speaking Arabic. They all wore the same uniform, a coverall with the word Bruxelles printed on the front, or at least that was all I could see.

The youngest looking man accepted a cup of hot tea. He said he was from North Africa and had a wife and two small children. He worked for the City of Brussels as a custodian of parks.

"Where are you from?" he asked me. "I'm from America, originally but I live in South Africa."

"Oh, where in America? California? New York?"

"No, nothing that exciting. I'm from Ohio."

"O-HIII-O," he said, as the letters made his mouth stretch in unfamiliar ways. "I don't know it."

"Not many do. It's OK."

We talked for forty minutes or so, refilling tea. He called some of his friends over to join us on their break.

They were curious about America. They wanted to know if I liked rap music. With the exception of 1990's Eminem, I couldn't say that I did. He learned to speak English by watching American movies. It took him about nine months, he said. "But I sound like Arnold Schwarzenegger."

Before long the conversation turned to the upcoming American presidential election. I had not returned to the US since the primaries, so I didn't really have much to say about the candidate, Donald Trump. He wanted to know if he would win.

"I don't see how," I replied. "He's a reality star, a business tycoon with no political experience."

He was not so sure. "He hates us. Trump. He hates us. If he becomes president of America, it will be hard."

He told me that since the subway attack, his wife had been ridiculed in public for her Muslim faith. She was afraid to be in public without him, not even in the grocery store. The kids were also afraid and hurt.

His eyes were wide open, looking at me as if I had some advice to bring home to her. I did not.

"I am so sorry that is happening to her. It must be so difficult." I said.

"It is hard. I can do nothing. She waits for me to finish with work before she even leaves the house," his voice broke just a bit, just long enough to catch my attention. We held each other's gaze, ever so briefly. He stopped talking, turned his head from my view, sipped his tea and kicked the bare patches of dirt with his work boots.

Soon, our hosts joined the conversation. They turned the conversation to religion, asking the men who they believe God is. There was much discussion about Allah, Abraham, and Elijah. Voices grew louder and postures defensive. I did not want to have this conversation.

These were the beautiful moments, standing face to face,

mirroring each other. I knew in my soul that I was made to create spaces for these conversations - space that is simple and sacred at the same time, caring and compassionate, but brimming with the possibility of transformation.

There is no program that could bring such restoration. It is held in the words whispered above the rim of coffee cups, in the space between people.

It is in these moments that seeds of reconciliation drop onto holy ground and silently, there grows a sanctuary between us.

41

Dichotomy

We recognize beauty for it somehow finds
reflection in us. It disrupts our indifference
and draws us to what is worth pursuing. It
opens us up to new possibilities as it
dissolves the borders between self
and other.

André Rabe

ONE AFTERNOON I walked three miles in the opposite
direction of what would soon be declared a state of emergency, or as some called it, "a war zone." Injustices I couldn't
understand were brimming, flagging me down for attention.

Tires were burning, roads were blocked, buses set on fire.
Stun guns, tear gas and water cannons were let loose. Fists in
the air, emboldened voices chanted while sirens wailed and
helicopters whirled overhead.

It wasn't that I didn't want to understand. I did. But my vision
is skewed by my privilege. Maybe I didn't have the right to

try to understand, but oh, my heart wanted to know. I hadn't yet earned the trust to merit an explanation.

So I turned in the opposite direction and walked to a beach-front art gallery filled with a different world. The smell of cappuccino and saltwater breezed through the exhibits. The water fountain bubbled outside, the leaves of the green palms waved melodically. The street was filled with laughter from a summer weekend, shopping bags from Boho stores, sunglasses and sundresses.

I sat there, irritated at the jolly, carefreeness of it all. The artwork stared at me. I wanted to climb inside the gold-framed Klimt and pretend.

The dichotomy of suffering and joy emptied out within a few steps of each other. It was not new, for it had always been. This day, the voices rose, agitated by one another. I wondered how to live in this - to be present in all of it.

MY FRIEND DEB, in Ohio, makes beautiful mosaics. She is also one of the kindest, most pure hearted people I know. I had to believe that when the glass and gemstones were being splintered and broken, and re-arranged by color, the pieces start thanking her for what she was about to create with them.

I believe we could live together, broken and re-arranged in a sculpture of beauty, cemented together by a creator who knows the beauty within each of us. But instead of dwelling in possibility with each other like the garden in Eden, we are too busy smoking the leaves from the Tree of the Knowledge of Good and Evil to see the toxic atmosphere enveloping us.

We get too high on our own judgment and self-righteousness to notice the rest of the garden.

Seeing others means seeing myself. If I only see others through the lens of the media or a Facebook post, I only see the mask - a fear intended to keep us apart. There is a part of me that is incomplete without your contribution. We need the perceived "other" to break out of an incestuous relationship with homogenized colonization and rampant fear-mongering. There is truly no "other." There is only us.

Since I had taught myself to be terrified, I could also learn to connect. If I had learned to be suspicious, I could also learn to trust. If I had taught myself to be defensive, I could also learn to be vulnerable. When we see face to face, we could see each other. We get a glimpse of one of God's best ideas wrapped in human flesh.

I cannot simply change my thinking, I must experience the change. I must live myself into a new thought, to paraphrase Henri Nouwen. I cannot ignore the pattern of my thinking, because that is me also. That is still part of me, my culture, my background, my experiences.

I can no longer compartmentalize it and hide it away, allowing it to suffocate. No, I must bring all of myself into the open for the redemptive purpose of renewal. The false belief began to fall away and a genuine understanding emerged in the light of truth, under the shade of the Tree of Life.

WEEKS after we arrived back in the US, we took a road trip that led us through St Louis, Missouri. When I saw signs for

Ferguson, I knew we just had to stop. It was a few weeks after the shooting death of Michael Brown by a police officer. I didn't know why, and certainly couldn't explain it, but I just knew, we had to stop. Despite Kevin's annoyance at the schedule deviation, he took the nearest exit into Ferguson.

We drove down the streets, saw the plywood boarded windows, the remnants of the riots and looting. I got out of the car, and walked down the street, looking for someone, anyone, that I felt I was "supposed" to meet.

In one of the most white privilege moves ever, I went to the place of torture and asked the people in pain to explain *my* feelings.

In graciousness, I found a young guy, a young father named Christopher, sitting on a street bench. He had escorted his mother to the grocery store and waited outside for her return. When she came out of the grocery store, he introduced us.

I can't tell you what transpired, but we were all in tears, holding hands, praying together in the middle of the sidewalk in Ferguson, Missouri.

I have learned there were conversations which needed to be had. There were things that needed to be said that aren't given space in the current system. It is in these places of protest where the words were boiling that I listened and listened only.

They allowed me in to feel, to see the raw hurts, the frustrations, the disappointments. I was there less than an hour. I left with a sliver of eternity.

When we only view people from a euthanized distance we miss the heartbeat. We miss humanity. We sit insulated from the life that flows from people. We miss so much when we look away from pain instead of running toward it. That's what Jesus would do if he walked through Ferguson - move toward an understanding of the pain with a hand reached out and not a finger pointing in judgment.

WHEN I SAT with Syrian women, all missing their husbands, trying to scratch out a living to feed their kids, I saw myself, a mother, a wife. They dropped their guards and let me see into their lives, into their horror. And they trusted me enough to share, to be worthy of carrying their story, now entwined with mine.

I talked to a Christian Palestinian woman who gave me freshly baked bread from her oven. She asked me what Americans thought of her. I honestly could not imagine that many Americans even knew she existed.

Seeing that I was unable to answer, she instead asked, How does snow feel on your skin?" "Was it really so cold?" She who was invisible to me, now was always visible, especially on cold nights when I feel the chill of winter in the air.

HOW CAN I experience unity without diversity? I can't. That's uniformity. Not all the crayons in the box are beige. I can't expect people to come to me. I must go. I need to leave my protected fortress and ignore the socialized safety sirens in my mind. I have to risk, to be hurt, to be misunderstood, to be rejected.

The olive branch of peace can feel like a prodding stick. Vulnerability levels the playing field. It's painful and risky to say, "I don't know why I'm here, I just needed to come to you," which is more authentic than to arrive at a place of hurting, assuming that I carry the remedy.

To see, I took off my blinders, let down my guard, and allowed myself to be seen. No answers, no solutions. Just a face turned toward pain, unflinching.

There were no questions to be asked because this was not an interrogation. There was only listening. There were no facts to be gathered because this wasn't a trial. There was only listening. There were no actions to be taken because this wasn't a project. There was only listening.

Listening is feeling, seeing, connecting, believing, hoping, growing. When I se myself in others, I become a better person. When others can see parts of themselves in me, there can be friendship.

Our culture told me that logically, I must choose, "either/or; us or them." But unity is not about choosing sides, one better or more truthful than the other. It is *both/and*. The line of division that forced a choice is what kept us living small.

Ubuntu. This South African phrase means, "I am because we are." It is community, relationship, and belonging.

We are all part of the whole. Our wholeness.

42

Welcome to Ocean View

We need, in every community, a group of
angelic troublemakers.

Bayard Rustin

THE BEST PART about the small Bible college I attended in
the early 90s, was that it was in downtown Chicago. We were
required to do "personal Christian ministry" once a week. I
usually was assigned to visit nursing homes which would
have been fine except I don't like the smell of nursing homes.

My favorite place to visit in Chicago was Cabrini Green, a
notorious public housing development. It was where my heart
came alive. It has since been torn down and the people relo-
cated, because you know, if one takes a building away, all the
problems disappear with it.

On one of the entrances to Cabrini Green, someone spray-
painted the words: *A bad seed under a bad moon.* I always
remembered that phrase. Hauntingly poetic, it was a self-

reflection that served as a warning to anyone making a wrong turn on their way to the Magnificent Mile.

Ocean View reminded me of Cabrini Green. What sprung from that ill-tended seed under a bad moon yielded murder, rape, incest, abuse, violence, drug addiction, and alcoholism to name a few rotting fruits.

Our area has the dubious distinction of having one of the highest rates of fetal alcohol births in the world. Years ago, the apartheid government allowed employers to pay their employees in cheap wine and alcohol, known as the DOP system.

That seed continues to bear fruit into future generations. There are dozens of shebeens (homemade breweries) in a community of 30,000 people but only policed by a handful of officers. Much like the homemade alchohol, crystal meth (tik), can be purchased cheaply and is easily accessible to all.

Ocean View began during the apartheid regime. Coloured residents were forcibly removed from their life-long homes and neighbors, and dumped, along with their belongings, in Ocean View. The castigated community, both the people and their pain, are hidden from sight to this day.

The government designated their former neighborhoods to be the property of "whites only." Some "white only" areas today are worth millions of dollars.

Ironically, the people were removed from areas with a stunning ocean view, to an area that has little view of the ocean, despite its name. The same mockery applies to other coloured areas in Cape Town like Lavender Hill, Grassy Park, and Sea Winds.

A South African friend said of Ocean View, "The community has had an alcohol dependence issue for generations, introduced as payment for work .... I have compassion for every mother in that community, teen or otherwise. Most of them have been raped, molested and abused in some way or another. I have compassion for the men in that community, teen or otherwise because finding good role models there are like finding hen's teeth."

Gangsterism can be deciphered by graffitied corners and drug deals in daylight. Twelve and thirteen-year old girls sleep with sugar daddies to get money for food and later become teenage mothers. Residents of Ocean View say the child hitmen, recruited to commit murders, are feared even though they are as young as nine-years-old.

The wounds in Ocean View are many, some visible, some not. It was birthed in apartheid's rejection. Ocean View is not a place that people visit unless you have a good reason. It doesn't draw people in like the majestic views and vineyards of their former homes.

It is here in Ocean View that God bends down close to the broken-hearted. We need Ocean View. They have much to say about the love of God.

When I am in Ocean View, I can see light. I see it pouring from the shattered windows of the flats. I see it in the vacant parking lots where men sit in small circles until sunset. I see it in the bright eyes of the children, the worn eyes of the mothers and the smiles that are returned to me each and every time I say hello.

Looking in from the outside, one might assume that Ocean View is a bad seed under a bad moon. That was the original intent, to contain and demoralize a minority group of people.

But this is the place of an arising. This is a place of hope. I feel it every time I enter. There is a rising, a shaking, an over-throwing about to take place. The tears and rage that have fertilized this ground are not silent.

There is redemption and reconciliation coming, not to Ocean view, but *from* Ocean View, to the rest of us. This is a home of wounded healers.

There is something special about this place, and not just the place, but the people. And not just any people, the women. And not just any women, the coloured women.

These coloured women will lead us into freedom, singing the songs of redemption, forgiveness and courage.

These are the women who could change a nation.

43

First We See Dimly, Then Face to Face

I am a slow unlearner. But I love my
unteachers.

Ursula K. LeGuin

AFTER AN EGG and avocado toast breakfast, I whisked the
boys out the door for school, yelling about exams and
studying and watching for cars when they crossed the street.
They were both 16-years-old but I'd been yelling that same
phrase for so many years, I couldn't stop now. It would be a
violation of mom codes everywhere.

*Across the valley in Ocean View, early morning gunshots sent
primary school-aged children running for the nearest shelter.
First and second-grade students, wearing green and grey
uniforms, socks pulled up to their knees, shook at the sound
of death in the air, burdened by oversized backpacks that
weighed them down as they ran.*

At the same time, I hopped into my car, cranked down the
windows, and turned on the music as I mentally prepared for

the daily schedule. I had to give several essential oil treatments scheduled for the first part of the day, then on to spending time with a few women for heart-to-heart chats, coffee with a friend, strategy meeting, dinner and, oh, yes, maybe I should stop at the grocery store on my way home to pick up something for dinner.

She waited in line at the taxi ranks, preparing for the long ride to the state hospital where her chemotherapy was scheduled for that day. She had to arrive early to get a place in line because the hospital served low-income families with government funding on a first come-first served basis. She waited six hours for her turn. When she was done enduring the trauma of cancer treatment alone, she took her place in a crowded taxi van for the long trip home, reeling from the chemotherapy and a claustrophobic load of people pressed into her.

We had a spare bedroom while our older three kids were traveling the globe. I opened the space to others who needed short term accommodation. We had a variety of guests but sometimes the bed remained unused and the room quiet.

She wouldn't stop talking, this one. She was my afternoon meeting. She talked and talked, on and on. Her family shared a one-bedroom place with her ex-husband and her ex-father-in-law. She slept in the kitchen. She didn't know if she'd ever lived in a place that was quiet and couldn't remember what it felt like to have privacy. Someday she would move to a place of her own. Someday.

I hung my laundry on the clothes line strung across the back of the house. The sun was late to make an appearance on that side of the house, so I was forced to wait for the afternoon sun to dry the laundry. My washing machine was small but reliable.

She scrubbed each child's school uniform by hand, then hung them in the bathroom, for fear of having them stolen should her neighbors see them strung on a clothesline in the open air. Each child had one school uniform. Immediately after school, they returned home to change clothes before daring to play. That uniform must last an entire year.

My boys came home from school around 1:30 pm. It was a standard South African school day. They attended school year round, so it all evened out I thought, since we didn't have a traditional American summer. One ambitious day, I was trying a new Pinterest-inspired muffin recipe with bananas and dark chocolate for an after-school snack. My boys didn't wear school uniforms because they attended an alternative school that was pushing the creative boundaries of education.

She asked me if I had some odd jobs for her to do, as her boys had nothing to eat last night and they would be home from school soon, with still nothing in their bellies.

I walked to the store to get a few supplies for dinner. I leisurely walked by myself, enjoying the fresh air. The store was filled with Christmas spirit. Gold and silver ornaments hung above the baked goods aisle, bells were jingling and the sweet smell of currants and candied citrus wafted through the bakery.

She walked to the store around the corner, knife hidden in her sleeve. She'd learned the hard way that purses and phones were ripe for thieves. Drug addicts wanted money and the value of human life was less than a pocket full of change. Arriving at the store, the clerk and all the merchandise stood behind caged walls, out of reach, away from grabbing hands. She made a verbal request from the cashier for an item, which he slipped through the hole in the metal wall upon payment.

When I walked through *her* neighborhood, there was little difference in each block, save maybe the exterior color which alternated from charcoal pink to soot yellow. Each block was connected by a nest of wires, from which pants, shirts, bed sheets, and bath towels were strung. The land was barren, with the exception of slim trunked trees fighting their way through cement mounds. The ground was sandy, bald and caked with the rubbish trampled underfoot.

Inside, the walls were cement blocks, painted yellow. Pictures of Jesus in various states of teaching and shepherding hung on the walls.

Her kitchen was quaint, fitted with a two-person table and a wooden cup rack. I couldn't imagine how 14 people ate in there, or how three different mothers fixed meals for their children. I smelled chicken curry, mixed with the smell of cigarettes and castille soap.

She grabbed my hands, winked, smiled wide at me, showing her gold tooth and I knew that despite the color of my skin, I was welcomed here.

Elvis Presley sang from a silver boom box sitting on an oak veneer coffee table. She took my hand, spinning and leading me in a joy-filled dance.

44

What a Strange Place for a Spa

Sawubona: [*sow:BOH:nah*] *an isiZulu
greeting directly translated means 'I
see you.'*

Sikhona: *[si:KOH:nah] an isi Zulu reply
directly translated means 'We are here to
be seen.'*

THIS WAS PROBABLY the last place on earth you'd expect to
find a spa experience on these sun-faded sheets under shattered windows. I can't say exactly when the idea took root. It
swirled around in my head after I was given a massage with
essential oils by my friend, Ginger, almost six years prior.

It was glorious, relaxing, calming and undoing. It was like a
cloud of lavender enveloped me and peppermint drop angels
fed me from golden bowls of carb-free manna.

These massages would do wonders I thought, for people in
South Africa, the land of constant traumatic stress disorders.

For the next few years, I thought about my experience, and how people deserved to be cared for just like that. It was one thing to provide physical needs like food, shoes, and toothbrushes, but that, that was something different.

Sure, most organizations adhere to Maslow and his needy hierarchy when helping others. But what about the emotional turmoil and stress that lodges in muscle and tissues and dismantles a person from the inside out? Who talked about that?

To uncover beauty, and gently nurse the wounds of the inner world back to life - this resonated within me. This was "missionary" work that didn't singe my own soul and reek of colonialism. I couldn't get this possibility out of my mind. But it only stayed there, in my mind, mounting an unrest and coup within my ideological framework.

On our second trip back to the US, two-and-a-half-years later, Ginger pampered me again with another essential oil massage and I instantly remembered the power of that experience and how effectual it would be for people living in trauma.

Irrationally, I decided it was now or never. I just *had* to take a class to learn a very specific type of healing touch called AromaTouch Technique[1] with essential oils. The day before we were to fly back to South Africa, I enrolled in this particular training in Columbus, Ohio.

I didn't know how I would use it, but I had a wild hunch that I needed to learn how to do this technique, which was quite inexplicable considering that I didn't like to touch feet.

At the last minute, Susie, the instructor, was able to make space in her training class. My friend, Grace, and I took the training together, just in case it was weird and I needed an escape partner.

The following day, we all boarded a plane back to Cape Town. Little did I know that this little decision would result in an incarnational shift in how I viewed life and compassion.

What was I doing? I had no clue, I just followed my intuition. I bought a used massage table, new sheets, bright throw pillows and cobbled together a "spa" room in Ocean View inside a small shipping container. That's right, a shipping container.

The windows had been shattered so many times that we just left them broken because as soon as they were repaired the vandals would start afresh. The jagged, broken glass did a number on the curtains as they blew in and out, shredding a little more with each inhale and exhale from the mighty Cape wind.

We opened the container each morning, not knowing what we would find inside. Large rocks, bullet holes, puddles of water from a June winter rain, remnants of someone breaking in and sleeping on the massage table overnight-anything was possible.

I thought I would start slowly, inviting people to come, sit and smell the relaxing oils while share their story. It wasn't technically called a massage, because, well it wasn't. However, for the purpose of cross-cultural explanations, I called it a massage. It sounded better than "oily rub down." It took just one massage for the word to spread throughout Ocean View that summer.

Auntie Liza hadn't been seen walking around the blokke for quite some time. Her spine curved and she hobbled at a slow pace, unsymmetrical. What was it that prompted Auntie Liza to come to a shipping container for a massage I couldn't say exactly. What was it that healed Auntie Liza so miraculously that she walked from flat to flat that day, dancing, proclaiming that something special happened to her? These massages were indeed, a living, compassionate prayer from within the creative womb of God.

"That is not a massage. No, it's not a massage. I was telling my neighbor, what happens is... healing. It's healing, that's what it is," said Auntie Liza to everyone she encountered. Word spread from woman to woman, as they gingerly and bravely walked into the container, not knowing what to expect, but hoping that Auntie Liza's words could be true.

The merciless sun blasted through the metal container and beads of sweat formed in places that I didn't know could sweat. Despite the external chaos and the shoddy conditions, these massages were indeed, an encounter that embraced the inner world with tangible compassion.

I often went home both exhausted and electrified from the loving encounter that I got to witness each day.

ONE DAY, after just finishing a massage, as I folded sheets and replaced lids on bottles, I heard gunshots and shrill screams outside our container. I peaked outside and saw people running in various directions, behind walls and around corners, ducking for cover. Mothers grabbed small children up into their arms and school-aged girls in green plaid uniforms and black patent shoes ran through an empty field for cover.

My immediate reaction was to duck below the windows, which was funny because I'm pretty sure bullets could go through this tin can of a shipping container. So my reaction to duck was instinctual, but pointless.

I tried to phone the police, but much to my chagrin, when I dialed, the call dropped because I had no airtime on my phone. This did not make me giggle. I said other things.

I waited until the place was quiet and the outside landscape seemed normal again before I poked my head up to see outside the glassless window. As if nothing had happened, people emerged from from the backside of buildings, shops and parked cars and resumed walking and chatting as if this was a minor disturbance.

After that experience, I worked out a new and improved emergency plan. The next time I heard gunshots, I would flip the massage table on its side, crouch behind it and inhale lavender like a pregnant woman in full labor.

ONE BY ONE, people inquired and bravely came to experience the unexpected. They arrived bearing the weight of combat but left with smiles, and tears of relief. Here, in the most unlikely of places, there was restoration - physically, emotionally, spiritually, psychologically. I saw it. I heard the stories.

There, with broken windows and no running water, in a metal box the sun set ablaze, with kids screaming, parents shouting and a call to prayer flowing through the gaping hole where window panes should be, there was a peace that whispered and wafted like the smell of evening primrose in full bloom.

. . .

I HEARD the wails of sorrow,

Of a mother whose murdered daughter was just buried,

Of the mother whose son pulled the trigger.

I heard the delightful sounds of snoring; the deep sleep of a grandmother who shared a bed with her daughter and her daughter.

I saw fresh bruises and heard the anguish from life with an abuser,

Tears of innocence lost in a place wild with rape,

I heard sounds of gratitude.

Of being heard and seen,

From a mother who shared a one bedroom flat with so many people that she slept in the kitchen.

I saw hope settle on a longing heart,

Drug addicts looking for an alternative and prodigals longing to return home.

WHERE SOULS AND PRAYER MET, the mystical arose and the planes of Heaven found fertile ground in which to unfurl seeds of outrageous love. Hurting people became vulnerable, offering their burden to be seen, to be shared, even just for a moment.

For a moment, I got to hold that sacred space, and looked into searching, aching, eyes to reflect back the love that I saw in them.

Here I was, invited to stand between pain and a holy whisper.

---

1. AromaTouch technique is a registered trademark of dōTERRA essential oils.

45

Chantel

God is everywhere around us and in us if only
we open our eyes. All the world is
beautiful if we have eyes to see the beauty,
for the world is packed with God.

Frank Laubach

I MET Chantel in a brief encounter on the streets of Ocean
View. After weeks of inviting her to come in for a massage,
she finally took me up on the offer. Her stress levels from
work were causing her to have painful headaches and to
behave crossly toward her kids, she said.

Despite shouldering a burden, she still swept into our
makeshift spa/shipping container like royalty, her head
wrapped in a champagne colored scarf, gold earrings
dangling. I wouldn't have been the least bit surprised had rose
petals fallen from the sky, marking her path and proclaiming
her entrance as she walked.

Her eyes smiled. Her nose was the most perfectly petite nose

I'd ever seen in my life. She is a majestic force. I could tell just by the way she carried herself.

I waited for her to prepare for a massage in the next room, the gentle music played from my phone in the background.

"I'm ready," she called from the room.

"How are you feeling?" I asked her as she anticipated her very first massage.

"Exposed."

As I dropped oils on her back, I could see her back shake with tears. I did not know what pain she carried, but I could see the locked places start to open; her muscles agreed to unclench as she began to release what was anchoring her. When emotion was given space to escape, this was often the result as the organs and muscles rejoiced in their deliverance.

As the massage ended, I quietly slipped out, covering her with a light blanket, leaving Chantel in an emotional cocoon. She remained quiet long after the massage, absorbed in the soothing silence, her body finally still.

She dressed and opened the door. She took a few steps toward me and collapsed on the couch as if the task of dressing drained all her energy. We sat on my little makeshift couch, propped up by bricks, covered with enough blankets and throw pillows to hide the second-hand stains. As we talked and processed the emotional release, she shared what had driven her there today, the last straw.

"It is allowed in Islam, you know. He told me only a few days ago. He is taking a second wife."

I nodded. That was not what I expected to hear. My mind

instantly flipped through a Rolodex of prepared responses which came up absolutely blank. The only thing I could do was stare and nod and encourage her to keep talking.

"He's so stupid. Why do I love him? He's so f*ing stupid."

Initially, she covered her mouth in feigned surprise at her language, but upon receiving no condemnation, continued on in the same pattern. Each time bringing more volume and more emotion.

She had two kids, not yet teens. She had no job, no place to stay, no family that would protest on her behalf. She'd lived a lifetime of shoulder shrugs and heavy sighs.

She was crying again.

I took her hands and asked if I could pray with her. She stopped crying and looked directly at me. I wasn't sure if she was going to get up and leave. But she just nodded and said, "I won't mind that."

I don't know what I prayed or if I even used words. I opened my eyes to see Chantel asleep, her head dropped onto her chest, still clutching my hand.

46

The Beginning

Those who sign on and depart the system of
anxious scarcity become the history
makers in the neighborhood.

Walter Brueggemann

FOUR YEARS PASSED since the massage idea took root and grew into a mist of peppermint and wild orange essential oil clouds that greeted people upon entering the door. We had not just one, but two containers.

My friend, Nadine, could pick up a twig and turn it into artwork, which is exactly what she did. The containers had unbreakable windows, covered by flowing curtains in translucent white.

The dingy, rusty, gray walls had been transformed into serene blue; a contrast to the newly laid white, wood floors. Succulents and greenery hung from macramé nests in every nook. Gentle music, throw pillows and cozy blankets awaited weary souls as they entered through life's divide.[1]

To get there, you had to walk a gravel path guided by low-lying weeds and ground covering, past crumbled cement buildings that have surrendered to graffiti, through smashed ginger beer bottles and blowing NikNak wrappers, over cigarette butts, and around the barbed wire fence into a displaced wonderland.

My sweet friend, Bernie, has a small café, right by our container. It serves as a little gathering place for those awaiting a massage or just in need of a listening ear and an understanding hug. She is a mother hen at heart, gathering her chicks to brood over each and every one.

I listened to Bernie retell the story of how one of the notorious gangsters from her block of flats came to her because he had a migraine headache. He asked if she had something that would help, so she rubbed his head with lavender, peppermint, and frankincense. He said he felt less pain immediately. That is exactly how the world will be changed-one revolutionary mother at a time.

In these past years, I've seen people experience physical healing. They arrived hurt and departed dancing. I've seen women come in with abuse written on their backs in black and blue and leave with courage, squared shoulders, back straight. I've seen gangsters come in with stab wounds and leave with a dream of opening a bakery.

People weren't coming because of *my* massages. They were coming because they were encountering God, laying down in green pastures, sitting by still waters, restoring their souls.

We needed a name for this…this community that hinged on nurturing, healing work in the midst of conflict and trauma. We decided to call it *Havilah Collective*. Havilah is a Hebrew word with several meanings - "to bring forth out of pain" and "to bring forth with dancing."

It is also in the book of Genesis:

A river flows out of Eden to water the garden and from there divides into four rivers. The first is named Pishon; it flows through Havilah where there is gold. The gold of this land is good. The land is also known for a sweet-scented resin and the onyx stone.[2]

A land of hidden gold and gemstones that was brought forth from pain and dancing - I can't think of a more fitting name to describe a sacred place of healing in unexpected places.

IN A POST-APARTHEID COMMUNITY founded on the forced removal of people based on the color of their skin, there is a treasure. It was already here. We were fortunate enough to have found it.

Two beautiful women from Ocean View stepped into their calling to take over the space, making it their own. Debbie and Isabel are the vision of transformation. Their personal stories of tragedy and triumph brought tears to my eyes in a tsunami of hope.

Through years of sharing our stories, our meals, and our pain, while encountering a God who loved us outrageously, we had formed a deep bond. They are formidable protectors and soothing mothers. Who they are is exactly who the community needs. They are the mothers who hold space and create beauty where there was none. Women healing women was one of the most powerful gifts to offer a broken world.

They not only had the heart capacity to heal their own community, but other ethnicities from our peninsula converged in this little container in Ocean View. When these women stretched out their hands to heal, there was a contagious current that drew people to them.

Women from affluent, gated communities booked appointments regularly with Debbie and Isabel. They didn't come to a shipping container for a spa experience, or to support a righteous cause. Massages can be found anywhere. No, a sacred space was found there; a space like none other.

As a group of ladies was leaving one day after massages with Debbie and Isabel and breakfast in Bernie's café, one beautiful Xhosa woman named Gloria turned and said, "I never, ever thought I would come *here* for healing, not Ocean View!"

In the most unlikely of places, was a piece of God's Kingdom, a sanctuary, a holy place. The healing we searched for came from the humblest of places. Whether it was a manger in Palestine or a shipping container in South Africa, both were birthplaces of liberation.

---

1. Funding for these projects was generously made possible by GiveOils.org, Paul and Betsy Holmes, and dōTERRA Healing Hands Foundation.
2. Genesis 2:10-12 The Message

47

Epilogue
SEVEN YEARS AFTER CHAPTER ONE...

We are all here for our own conversion.

Edwina Gateley

I WAS SITTING in a Benedictine Monastery in Northern Ireland known for peace and reconciliation work. Directly across the table from me sat Brother Thierry, a monk who slightly resembled Phil Collins.

His hairline was a horseshoe shape of average brown. Small, rectangular glasses dangled from the tip of his button nose. He was draped in creme colored robes that didn't quite hide his white tube socks and Birkenstock sandals. He was dropping pearls of wisdom in a soft, French accent.

"What right does any one of have to make someone else's life a living hell?" Brother Thierry peered over his glasses and said, "We carry Christ. To look at someone else and to meet another being is an exchange of gifts."

That was exactly what I had experienced in the seven years

after leaving America - an exchange of gifts. The storytellers I met have shaped me, taught me, pained me, pruned me and forged the path to becoming. I needed generous gift-givers who both extended the invitation to arrive on far shores and those who accepted the invitation to leave safety's side.

I will continue to search for those who are willing to celebrate the gifts in all of us, who are here to form communities that remind us that we are all deeply loved.

Imagine what the world will be like when we make space for these bringers and bearers of reconciliation and hope.

May we all be reconcilers and celebrants, carrying the good news within our bones.

Where there is certainty, may we find wonder.

Where there is pride, may we learn humility.

Where there is comfort, may we kindle resistance.

Where there is pain, may there be transfiguration.

Acknowledgments

To my sweet friends who volunteered to correct me: Amy Townsend, Marcy Hintz, Heidi Isaacs, Deby Aho, Simone Weaver, Nicole Keisler and Shawn Hain. Thank you for turning this mess into an encouragement.

I wouldn't still be writing if it weren't for my friend Amy Wrench. She began correcting my grammar in college and I've loved her ever since.

Thank you to Paul and Betsy Holmes for believing that Ocean View is worth the investment. Thank you to Matt and Sara Janssen for creating space for me to breathe. You are our oxygen tank.

Thank you to Tenille and to Ginger, my Ohio roots, who started me down this path.

Thank you to Kevin for reading and re-reading the same story endless times without complaint.

Thank you to my kids, Jackson, Dylan, Evangeline, Hudson, and Ethan for enduring this seemingly endless project, and for jumping into the deep end with us. You are my main characters.

I am forever changed by the sweet souls in Ocean View who invited me into their world: to Johann, Bernie, Isabel, Debbie, Marion, Ishiqua and everyone at the Ocean View Care Centre and Havilah Collective, thank you. You are the ultimate storytellers.

About the Author

Christina Quist is passionate about reconciliation and conflict transformation through holistic and nurturing activism. This is her first book.

She enjoys dry humor, essential oils, and the Enneagram. She lives in Cape Town, South Africa with her husband Kevin, their twin boys, and a cat named Egg. Her three adult children live in various places around the world.

She can be contacted via Facebook, Instagram or email: Christina@thequists.com

To order essential oils and support Havilah Collective, visit: www.mydoterra.com/havilahcollective

Made in the USA
Columbia, SC
19 December 2019